CANNABIS COOKBOOK

Quick and Simple Medical Marijuana Edible Recipes

BY JOSEPH BOSNER

Cannabis Cookbook

© Copyright 2019 - All rights reserved.

The content contained within this book may not be reproduced, duplicated or transmitted without direct written permission from the author or the publisher.

Under no circumstances will any blame or legal responsibility be held against the publisher, or author, for any damages, reparation, or monetary loss due to the information contained within this book. Either directly or indirectly.

Legal Notice:

This book is copyright protected. This book is only for personal use. You cannot amend, distribute, sell, use, quote or paraphrase any part, or the content within this book, without the consent of the author or publisher.

Disclaimer Notice:

Please note the information contained within this document is for educational and entertainment purposes only. All effort has been executed to present accurate, up to date, and reliable, complete information. No warranties of any kind are declared or implied. Readers acknowledge that the author is not engaging in the rendering of legal, financial, medical or professional advice. The content within this book has been derived from various sources. Please consult a licensed professional before attempting any techniques outlined in this book.

By reading this document, the reader agrees that under no circumstances is the author responsible for any losses, direct or

Cannabis Cookbook

indirect, which are incurred as a result of the use of information contained within this document, including, but not limited to, — errors, omissions, or inaccuracies.

Cannabis Cookbook

Table of Contents

INTRODUCTION IX

CHAPTER ONE ABOUT CANNABIS 1
- Difference between THC and CBD 3
  - What exactly is THC? 3
  - The medical applications of THC 3
  - What is CBD? 4
  - The medical applications of CBD 4

CHAPTER TWO ABOUT CANNABIS EDIBLES 6
- Purchasing Cannabis 10

CHAPTER THREE ALL ABOUT CBD 14
- Cannabis 15
- Hemp 15
- Cannabinoids 15
- CBD 15
- THC 16
- Psychoactive 16
- Which States Allow Oil Production In The CBD? 19

CHAPTER FOUR BENEFITS OF CANNABIS 21
- Slows Down Cancer 21
- Prevention of Alzheimer's 22
- Treating Glaucoma 22
- Reducing Arthritis 23
- Epileptic Seizures 23
- Soothing Tremors 24
- Crohn's Disease 24
- Dravet's Syndrome 25
- Quitting Smoking and Drug Withdrawal 25
- Anxiety Disorders 25
- Reduces the Side Effects of Hepatitis C 26
- Reducing the Side Effects of Chemotherapy 26
- Acne 26

DIABETES	27
FIBROMYALGIA	27

CHAPTER FIVE SIDE EFFECTS OF CANNABIS 28

CHAPTER SIX CALCULATING THC DOSAGE 31

CHAPTER SEVEN INTRODUCTION TO DECARBOXYLATION 34

ABOUT DECARBOXYLATION	34
STEPS FOR DECARBOXYLATING CANNABIS AT HOME	35

CHAPTER EIGHT COOKING WITH CANNABIS 37

CANNABIS CAN TASTE GOOD	37
NOT LIMITED TO HEAVY FOODS	37
SELECT THE RIGHT STRAIN	38
YOU CAN COMBINE IT WITH ALCOHOL	38
INCLUDE IT IN YOUR MEAL	39
PREPARE IT BEFOREHAND	39
TRY DOING IT YOURSELF	40
TIPS FOR TROUBLESHOOTING	40
Don't grind it too much	*40*
Add water while infusing cannabis	*41*
Cooking at a high temperature	*41*
Always decarb cannabis	*42*
Adding too much marijuana	*42*
Adding too little	*43*
Cleanliness matters	*43*
Sweet and savory recipes	*43*
Control heat	*44*
Choose wisely	*44*

CHAPTER NINE CANNABIS-INFUSED BASIC RECIPES 46

HOW TO DECARB CANNABIS:	46
CANNABIS TINCTURE	46
CANNABUTTER / MARGARINE	48
CANNABIS-INFUSED COOKING OIL	49
CANNA-FLOUR	50
CANNABIS MILK	52
MARIJUANA HONEY	53

WEED SUGAR	54
COCONUT CANNABIS OIL	55
CANNABIS MAYONNAISE	56
CANNABIS PEANUT BUTTER	57
CANNA-CREAM CHEESE	58
MARIJUANA VINAIGRETTE	59

CHAPTER TEN MUNCHIES 60

SWEET POTATO FRIES	60
WEED BISCUITS	62
BAKED APRICOT BRIE	65
CANNABIS GRANOLA	67
SUPER LEMON HAZE MEXICAN GUACAMOLE	69
STUFFED MINI PEPPERS	70
MONSTER MUNCHIE BALLS	73
HIALEAH HASH BROWNS	74

CHAPTER ELEVEN BREAKFAST RECIPES 75

BANANA NUT BREAD	75
WEED FRENCH TOAST	78
KRISPY KREME DOUGHNUTS	80
BREAKFAST "BAKED" BURRITOS	83
CANNA-SCRAMBLER	85
CANNABIS BREAKFAST EGG CUPS	86
CANNA-CHEESY EGG BENEDICT	89
DENVER OMELET	91
OATMEAL PANCAKES	92
POTFFLES (MEDICATED WAFFLES)	94
WEED BREAD	95
QUINOA CORN CANNABIS MUFFINS	97
BREAKFAST SANDWICHES	99
CANNABIS COFFEE CAKE	101
CAFÉ DE CANNABIS	103

CHAPTER TWELVE LUNCH RECIPES 104

MARIJUANA AVOCADO SHAKE	104
BANANA AND STRAWBERRY SMOOTHIE INFUSED WITH CANNABIS	105

Cannabis Cookbook

    Cannabis Vegetable Tart 106
    Smoked Mac 'n' Cheese 108
    Spinach Cannabis Quiche 111
    Weed Ramen Noodles 113
    Marijuana Meatloaf 114
    Raspberry Pear Grilled Cheese Sandwich 116
    Ham and Cheddar Panini 118
    Cannabis Mango-Cashew Fried Rice 120
    Vegan Cannabis Spaghetti Bolognese 123
    Weed Quesadillas 125
    Laid-Back Latkes 128

CHAPTER THIRTEEN DINNER RECIPES 130
    Baked Shrimp Scampi 130
    Broccoli Cheddar Casserole 132
    Cannabis-Infused Turkey Bolognese 134
    Rasta Pasta 136
    Rib Eye with Chimichurri Sauce 138
    Chicken Pic-Canna 140
    Chicken Pot-cciatore 142
    Cannabis Chicken Pot Pie 144
    Gnocchi in Ganja Butter 146
    Dope Dumplings Vegetable Casserole 149
    Classic Cannabis Lasagna 152
    Pesto Cannabis Pizza 155
    Cannabis Mashed Potatoes 158
    Chicken and Vegetables Thai Curry 159
    Cannabis Tuna Steaks with Sautéed Spinach 161
    Lobster Étouffée 163
    Cannabis Fish Tacos 165

CHAPTER FOURTEEN SOUP AND SALAD RECIPES 167
    Pumpkin Potato Soup 167
    Fresh Tomato Soup 169
    Cannabis Quinoa Stew 171
    Chili Con Cannabis 173
    Split Pea and Carrot Soup 175

- Butternut Squash Soup ... 177
- Medicated French Onion Soup ... 179
- Cannabis Chicken Noodle Soup ... 182
- Cannabis Cabbage Salad with Sesame-Lime Dressing ... 184
- Butternut Squash and Kale Salad ... 186
- Cranberry Walnut Salad ... 188
- Kale Salad with Cannabutter Vinaigrette ... 190
- Cannabis-Infused Greek Salad ... 191

CHAPTER FIFTEEN DESERT RECIPES ... 193
- Pineapple Express Upside-Down Cake ... 193
- Banana Marijuana Ice Cream ... 196
- Dank Cheesecake ... 198
- Cannabis Caramels ... 202
- Pumpkin Cheesecake Smoothie ... 203
- Marbled Marijuana Brownie Bars ... 205
- No-Bake Almond-Butter Canna-Cookies ... 207
- Cannabis Peanut Butter Fudge ... 209
- Piña Co-Canna Pie Cake ... 210
- Raspberry Peach Cannabis Cobbler ... 212
- Pot Pastelitos ... 215

CONCLUSION ... 217

Cannabis Cookbook

INTRODUCTION

I want to thank you for choosing this book, *Cannabis Cookbook – Quick and Simple Medical Marijuana Edible Recipes,* and hope you find the book helpful in gathering all the information you need to understand cannabis and how it can be used in cooking.

There are different ways in which you can consume cannabis, and the most popular form is cannabis edibles. Yes, you can cook with cannabis! It is quite easy to cook with cannabis, provided you are armed with the appropriate information. If you want to learn how to cook with cannabis, then this is the right book for you. This is a detailed guide on cooking with one of the most popular ingredients—cannabis! Before you get started, there are a couple of things that you must know. For instance, what is the ideal personal dosage, and how can you measure the potency of cannabis? What are the common mistakes that beginners make while cooking with it and the ways you can avoid them? Well, if you want to learn about all this, along with other things, then you have chosen the right book.

In this book, you will learn about cannabis edibles, the health benefits they offer, the things to keep in mind while buying and cooking with cannabis, and the different tips you can use to troubleshoot any issues while cooking with cannabis. Apart from all this, you will find various recipes to cook cannabis edibles. The recipes given in this book are quite simple and easy to understand. You merely need to gather all the ingredients that you need, follow the recipes, and voila! Within no time you will be able to start cooking cannabis edibles quite easily!

So, let us get started without any further ado!

Cannabis Cookbook

CHAPTER ONE

ABOUT CANNABIS

Cannabis, marijuana, or weed, regardless of the name, has quite a long history of human usage. Evidence shows that most ancient civilizations used to cultivate the cannabis plant for the various medicinal benefits it offers. The cultivation of this plant can be dated back to around 500 BC in Asia. The history of cannabis use in the western regions dates back to the early colonists in America, who used to grow hemp plants for making textiles and ropes. The hemp plant was originally cultivated in the regions of Central Asia before it was brought to Africa, Europe, and the Americas. Hemp plants not only grow quickly, but they have different uses as well, and this is the reason why cannabis was widely cultivated in the regions of colonial America and the Spanish missions. The early strains of the hemp plants had a low level of tetrahydrocannabinol (THC). Some evidence also suggests that the cultivators were aware of the psychoactive properties of the hemp plant.

There are various strains of the cannabis plant, and they can be widely classified as cannabis indica, cannabis sativa, and cannabis ruderalis. The popular use of cannabis as a recreational drug because of the high levels of THC found in some strains is the reason why there are strict rules about its cultivation. However, it doesn't mean that cannabis doesn't have any health benefits. In fact, the use of cannabis for medical purposes has become quite popular, and it has been legalized in different countries.

Sir William Brooke O'Shaughnessy, an Irish doctor who was studying in India during the 1830s, discovered that extracts of the marijuana plant could be used to reduce pain and nausea in those suffering from cholera. By the late 1800s, cannabis extracts were sold in doctors' clinics and pharmacies throughout the USA and Europe for treating stomach ailments and other problems. Different studies that were conducted later showed that the compound THC is responsible for the different benefits marijuana offers. Not just the medicinal benefits, but also the psychoactive effects of marijuana are caused because of THC.

The widespread use of cannabis as a recreational drug was rather alarming, and this led to its prohibition by the government. In fact, the Controlled Substances Act of 1970, enacted under President Richard Nixon, prohibited the use of cannabis. Once people started to realize the various medicinal benefits that cannabis offers, there was pressure from different groups to legalize the use and cultivation of marijuana. Cannabis can be used to alleviate the unbearable and painful symptoms of different chronic ailments like cancer, arthritis, and so on. The growing popularity of cannabis as a substitute for pharmaceutical painkillers led to the introduction of different reforms for the legalization of cannabis within the US for medical purposes. In fact, the first state to legalize the use of cannabis for medical purposes was California. Since 2018, medical marijuana has been legalized in a lot of states in the US. However, the laws about the legalization of marijuana keep changing, and therefore, I suggest that you always go through the laws of your state before you start using marijuana in any form.

The two different types of cannabinoids that are naturally present in the resin of the marijuana plant (cannabis sativa) are tetrahydrocannabinol (referred to as THC) and cannabidiol (CBD). These substances tend to react with the cannabinoid receptors present in the body. However, there are different effects that are brought about by these components. This is the reason why CBD is preferred in medical treatment over THC.

Difference between THC and CBD

What exactly is THC?

The main psychoactive ingredient present in the marijuana plant is referred to as THC. This is the agent that is primarily responsible for creating the feeling of being "high" that is associated with the use of marijuana. This compound works by replicating the effects of anandamide. Anandamide is a neurotransmitter that is produced naturally in the human body and it helps to modulate sleeping and eating habits as well as the perception of pain by the mind.

The main effects of THC include feelings of relaxation, altered senses (smell, sight, and hearing), fatigue, hunger, and reduced aggression.

The medical applications of THC

Research conducted for understanding the medical applications of THC show that it might be useful in:

- Reducing the various side effects of chemotherapy, like nausea and vomiting, along with improving appetite

- Helping treat multiple sclerosis by easing painful spasms while improving bladder function

- Helping to relieve pressure in the eyes of people with glaucoma

- Alleviating certain symptoms of AIDS by increasing appetite

- Reducing tremors experienced in cases of spinal injury.

What is CBD?

The chemical formulas of THC and CBD are the same. However, the atoms are arranged differently in CBD. This slight variation is what enables THC to create a psychoactive effect, whereas CBD doesn't do this. About 40 percent of cannabis extract is constituted of CBD. There is plenty of it that's available in nature, and this, coupled with the fact that it doesn't make the user "high," makes it a good candidate for medical use.

The main effects of CBD include the reduction of psychotic symptoms, reduction in levels of anxiety, reduction in inflammation, and relief from convulsions as well as nausea.

The medical applications of CBD

Research shows that CBD can be quite helpful to reduce the psychotic symptoms caused due to schizophrenia and helps manage social anxiety disorder by reducing the levels of anxiety. It can be successfully used for treating depression by decreasing depressive symptoms in an individual. It can also be used for managing the side effects of cancer treatments by stimulating appetite and reducing pain and nausea.

Cannabis Cookbook

CHAPTER TWO

ABOUT CANNABIS EDIBLES

What are cannabis edibles? Food that is infused with cannabinoids is referred to as a cannabis edible. Edibles come in different forms like brownies, cookie dough, and so on. It is a popular notion that cannabis can only be added to sweet treats. Well, this might be a popular notion, but it is nothing more than a misconception. You can use cannabis-infused oil or butter in any recipe that calls for regular oil or butter. So, any food, regardless of whether it is sweet or savory, that is infused with cannabinoids is referred to as an edible.

There are different forms in which cannabis edibles are available. Cannabis edibles can be made in the form of brownies, candies, chocolates, cookies, drinks, popcorn, and so on. You will find various recipes for cannabis edibles in this book. Edibles don't have to be restricted to desserts and can be in the form of savory items too. A lot of readily available cannabis edibles look like regular foods. So, you need to carefully go through the labels of the products you purchase. Also, you need to store edibles in a cold and dark place without any moisture. Please store the cannabis edibles such that they are out of the reach of children and pets.

You might be wondering if cannabis edibles have the same effect as smoking edibles. This is a common concern. To put it simply, the effect of consuming edibles is quite different from smoking cannabis. In fact, when you smoke cannabis, it has an instantaneous effect, while cannabis edibles can take a while to start working. It usually takes about 30 minutes to up to two hours for cannabis edibles to take effect. Also, the effects of cannabis edibles usually last longer than smoking.

Another question that a lot of people have is why cannabis edibles seem to have a stronger effect. The quantity of THC present in cannabis edibles is quite varied. This is one reason why it becomes rather difficult to keep track of the amount of THC a user consumes. The THC content in homemade cannabis edibles tends to be quite varied. A lot of users are caught unawares by the potency and long-lasting effects that edibles have.

So, who can buy cannabis edibles? Different states have different rules about the purchase and legality of cannabis edibles. There isn't a uniform law about the legality of cannabis, at least not yet. For instance, medical, as well as retail cannabis is legalized in Colorado. In Denver, any individual who is at least 21 years old can legally purchase and use retail cannabis. Before you start using cannabis in any form, please ensure that its use is legalized in the state that you live in. After all, ignorance of the law is not a defense! The use of cannabis is not advisable for pregnant women and minors.

Edibles are also known as medibles, and these items usually contain THC. Activated cannabis refers to oils or plant materials whose psychoactive properties are heat-activated. These psychoactive substances are the reason why a person experiences a "high" after consuming cannabis edibles. Edible cannabis treats have been used by humans for hundreds of years. In fact, in some places in Eastern Europe, a popular form of medicine was candies infused with cannabis. Also, in India, a drink made with cannabis, known as bhang, is quite popular. The history of this drink dates back to around 2000 BC. Bhang is made with psychoactive cannabis and has been used for a long time for spiritual and medicinal reasons. In western countries, cannabis is usually infused into a variety of treats and isn't limited to just a couple of items.

Cannabis edibles are quite different from all the other forms of cannabis that are available. Cannabis edibles are preferred over other means because their effects last for longer. Ingesting cannabis gives a different experience than inhaling it. Edibles are stronger, and the psychoactive high that they give is more potent. The potency of cannabis edibles can come as a pleasant surprise to even regular users of cannabis.

So, how long does it take for edibles to produce the desired effect? If you are inhaling cannabis, then you can experience its psychoactive effects within no time. However, edibles need a while longer. The amount of time before cannabis edibles take effect will vary from one individual to another. This is the reason why it is important to get the dosage of THC in cannabis right. The metabolic rate of your body, whether you are consuming cannabis after a meal or 0n empty stomach, along with several other factors, influences the time that edibles need to take effect. Since it takes a long time for its activation, it is advisable that you give your body at least an hour or two before you increase the dosage of the edibles. Once you realize the way cannabis affects your body, you can start increasing or decreasing the dosage of cannabis accordingly.

Edibles not only take a while to take effect, but their effect also tends to last for up to six to seven hours if the right dosage has been administered. If you consume a rather large amount of cannabis edibles, then the effects of cannabis might still be felt for up to 24 hours. A high dosage of cannabis means that on the following day you might experience lethargy, mild headaches, and even some fatigue. If you feel like your motor skills have slowed down slightly, that's also a potential side effect of the residual cannabis in your system and will wane in a couple of hours.

Why are edibles considered to be more potent than the other forms of marijuana? To put it simply, this is because edibles are metabolized by the body and this makes them more potent. When you smoke or inhale cannabis, then the psychoactive ingredient in cannabis, THC, is absorbed by the lungs, and from there it enters the bloodstream. Once it enters the bloodstream, it is transported to fatty tissues present in the body like the brain, wherein the psychoactive ingredient connects with the receptors present in the cells.

However, when you eat cannabis edibles, then the edibles need to be digested in the stomach and the intestinal tract. Apart from this, the edibles also need to be metabolized by the different enzymes in the liver before you can start experiencing the effects of consuming cannabis edibles. The enzymes present in the liver will start breaking down the THC present in cannabis. When THC is synthesized in this manner, the resultant product is 11-hydroxy-THC. This compound is more potent than THC. The 11-hydroxy-THC is smaller than THC and enters brain cells more easily than regular THC. All this takes some time and therefore, cannabis edibles take a while longer to take effect than other forms of cannabis.

Another question that worries cannabis users is whether one can overdose on edibles. Well, it is not likely that one can have a fatal overdose by consuming cannabis. However, this doesn't mean that there are no side effects of consuming large dosages of cannabis. Consuming large quantities of cannabis might lead to the user experiencing discomfort for a couple of hours. Some negative side effects of consuming cannabis include paranoia, drowsiness, red eyes, dryness of the mouth, and anxiety. You will learn more about the short-term and long-term side effects of consuming cannabis in the coming chapters. The only thing that you can do if you have accidentally consumed a large dosage of cannabis edibles is to wait it out. You need to sit tight and wait for the symptoms to fade away.

There are a couple of things that you can do to counteract an intense high that you might experience if the dosage of cannabis edibles is high. You can try distracting yourself by listening to relaxing music or even by sleeping. Experts also suggest that chewing on fresh peppercorns can help to ease some of the anxiety that THC induces. Apart from this, you can also try taking some CBD to counteract the THC in your system. Instead of doing all this, I suggest that you start with a small dosage, especially if you have never consumed cannabis edibles before. Always listen to your body when you are using cannabis in any form.

It might happen that you don't feel any of the effects of cannabis edibles that you consume. Do you know why this happens? This might be due to something referred to as first-pass metabolism. At times the enzymes present in the liver start cleaning out compounds that they deem to be unnecessary and in this process, the enzymes might get rid of the THC as well. Instead of metabolizing the THC, this compound is altogether eliminated from the body. The first-pass metabolism can reduce or even completely eliminate the effects of cannabis. In fact, this is the reason why some people tend to need a higher dosage of cannabis than others. To counteract this mechanism, please ensure that you eat something before consuming the cannabis edibles. In fact, it is a good idea to have a fatty meal so that the THC can be easily metabolized. THC is fat- soluble and if you have some fat readily available in your system, it will be easier for your body to metabolize the THC from the cannabis you ingest. You must always wait for at least two hours to allow the THC in the cannabis to be activated. So, even if you don't feel like the cannabis is working, wait for at least two hours before you consume some more.

Purchasing Cannabis

Before you can start cooking cannabis edibles at home, there is another important step that you must not skip. Are you wondering what this step is? Well, you do need to buy the plant material before

Cannabis Cookbook

you can start cooking, don't you?

So the first thing that you must ensure is that cannabis has been legalized in your state. If you happen to reside in a state where legal cannabis is available, then you can get started. In this section, you will learn about where you can buy legal cannabis.

The first thing that you need to do is find a cannabis dispensary! For purchasing cannabis, you need to be at least 21 years old and must have a valid ID. A quick Google search will help you find all the legal cannabis dispensaries within your neighborhood. You can also use several online store locator tools for finding cannabis dispensaries. You can also check the online reviews of the dispensaries! You can explore a couple of different shops since each dispensary will have different products available. Once you find a dispensary that you are happy with, the next thing you ought to do is learn about the cannabis basics. You can always ask the staff at the dispensary for suggestions, but I suggest that you do a little research by yourself. So take some time out of your schedule and read about the different strains of cannabis and the recommended dosage of THC that you need. By doing this basic research, you will be able to make an informed decision.

Once you do all this, it is time to pick up the cannabis item that you need. You can purchase cannabis flowers, readymade edibles, concentrates, pre-rolls, and even other types of cannabis body products.

Now that you know what cannabis edibles are and the ways in which you can buy them, the next question that you might be wondering about is the cost of cannabis edibles! Edibles can be a rather cost-effective means of consuming cannabis, but all this depends on your level of tolerance as well as the options that are available at the local dispensary. The cost of one gram of cannabis flowers can be as high as $20 per gram, and this depends on the area where you live. The cost of edibles primarily depends on the kind of product you are purchasing and the type of edible you want to buy. At times, dispensaries have sales on specific products. As with any other food item, the cost of readymade cannabis edibles depends on the ingredients that are used, along with the type of cannabis that has been used. The cheapest available option for cannabis edibles is cannabis-infused caramels that can cost anywhere between $1 and $3.

Cannabis Cookbook

CHAPTER THREE

ALL ABOUT CBD

What is cannabidiol? Cannabidiol or CBD is a natural substance found in the cannabis plant that has recently attracted attention for various reasons. Cannabidiol is a relatively new discovery and therefore has still not been thoroughly researched. The results gathered so far from all the research are rather promising. However, there is a lot of misinformation around this topic. The popularity of CBD oil is definitely growing, as is its use.

Since the use of CBD oil is relatively new, there are still some loopholes in terms of impact. In this section, you will learn the basics of cannabidiol.

Where does the CBD come from? Hemp is a specific strain of cannabis and is used to extract cannabidiol. The cannabis plant contains about 85 different types of cannabinoids and CBD is one of them. CBD is the second most common compound in hemp and makes up about 40 percent of extracts. This is where all the confusion starts.

Another common ingredient in cannabis is THC. THC is an intoxicating compound and is responsible for the "high" that users experience. There is a lot of stigma associated with using CBD. This stigma is the result of the simple fact that people consider CBD THC. All these concerns are unfounded, but to some extent understandable, especially since all the terminology used in connection with the CBD may be very confusing.

Here are a couple of terms that you must be familiar with while dealing with cannabis.

Cannabis

It is a flowering plant. The three different types of cannabis are ruderalis, indica, and sativa. Cannabis not only has medicinal applications, but industrial ones too. Cannabis has been used for ages for its tough fiber, oils, and other medicinal uses. However, it is also a very popular recreational drug and therefore the cultivation of marijuana is strictly regulated since some strains of cannabis tend to have high levels of THC.

Hemp

It is a commonly available variety of cannabis and is solely used for its fiber, seeds, and oils. Hemp can be transformed into a variety of products like wax, cloth, pulp, resin, paper, rope, oil, and even fuel.

Cannabinoids

This term refers to naturally and artificially created chemical substances. There are various cannabinoids and they all have different effects—there are some that have a calming and a relaxing effect whereas the rest are categorized as illegal drugs.

CBD

CBD is a naturally occurring chemical in a cannabis plant and is the second most abundantly available constituent of a marijuana plant.

CBD is legalized and is safe for consumption but is still confused with THC.

THC

The most abundant component of a marijuana plant is THC, a psychoactive cannabinoid. This is responsible for the high that the users experience when smoking cannabis and therefore, the use and production of THC are strictly regulated.

Psychoactive

If a chemical compound can directly affect the central nervous system, then it is said to be psychoactive. There are various medical uses for psychoactive substances. In fact, they are used in anesthetics, psychiatric drugs, and so on, but some of these substances are purely used for recreational purposes, can have a variety of side effects, and are highly addictive.

It is a common misconception that CBD oil can make a user experience the feeling of being "high." This is nothing but a misunderstanding. CBD is not psychoactive and does not affect your mental functions. In other words, CBD can in no way have any sort of effect on your mental functions, so you will not feel high or like you are stoned even when you consume a lot of CBD-oil-infused products.

You might be wondering why this happens. Well, only cannabis plants grown specifically for high levels of THC will make you feel like you are high. However, not all cannabis plants are the same, and there are other cannabinoids in the plant besides THC. Some plants are bred solely because of the high amount of CBD and are known as hemp. Hemp plants have only traces of THC (less than 0.3 percent). The combination of high levels of CBD in combination with nonexistent

Cannabis Cookbook

levels of THC does not make CBD products derived from cannabis psychoactive.

Now, you may wonder, if CBD does not make you high, then what does it do? Without going into depth about the different technical aspects of the way CBD functions, here is a brief explanation of what CBD does. CBD affects several receptors in your body, instead of directly binding your cannabinoid receptors such as THC; CBD has an indirect effect on these receptors and increases the number of endocannabinoids produced in the body. This causes the user to feel relaxed when CBD oil products are ingested or vaped. When CBD-based products are used topically, the pain, swelling, or discomfort in a particular area are reduced. The effects of CBD are quite mild and are limited to impacting unpleasant symptoms that torment you, without interfering with your daily life.

Many CBD users worry that even after 30 minutes of using CBD oil, they will not feel differently and wonder if it works or not. Well, give CBD an hour, and you will almost forget all about any sort of discomfort that you were previously experiencing. With CBD, you will not feel like you are high. All it does is relieve pain.

CBD is used to relieve pain, anxiety, and is also at times used in lieu of a sleeping pill. So, is CBD a drug or not? Yes, CBD is cannabinoid. Is CBD found in drug tests? Even if it is used for the right reasons, any drug that shows up in a drug test does not spell good news.

To answer your question, it is very unlikely that any traces of CBD will appear in a drug test. Most of the drug tests that are administered are designed to pick up any trace amounts of THC and not CBD. CBD is a chemical substance, and as soon as you take it, it is broken down by your body. The average drug test is not so complicated that, unlike THC, it can detect traces of CBD. CBD is chemically different from THC, and no pure CBD is detected. However, most cannabis-derived CBD products usually contain traces of THC.

Even if the CBD oil contains only a small amount of THC, will you pass a drug test? There are several types of drug tests, each with different detection thresholds. Even if your CBD oil contains traces of THC, this is impossible to prove in a drug test. There is no standardized test for CBD, and a special test is required. So, if you are worried about any upcoming drug tests at your workplace, you don't have to worry. The employer must specifically designate a test that can detect CBD. All this is just an extra cost for the employer. Since CBD is not psychoactive, it does not adversely affect the body's nervous or musculoskeletal system. Thus, you do not need to worry about CBD negatively affecting your life.

The legality of CBD oil is a rather complex subject. With the increasing efforts to legalize medical marijuana, it is important to understand which aspects of cannabis are and are not legalized.

In the US, nine states have legalized the use of marijuana for recreational purposes. The main reason for the legalization of the CBD, one of the cannabinoids, is that it has several therapeutic purposes. The most popular form of CBD is CBD oil. It is a combination of CBD extract and carrier, such as coconut oil, that can be swallowed or evaporated. Legalizing marijuana is a rather dismal topic where you have to deal with federal and state laws. The legality of CBD oil can be complex. Let's look at the legality of the CBD oil.

Is CBD oil legal at the federal level? Although many states have legalized various forms of marijuana, the US Drug Enforcement Administration (DEA) still classifies CBD as a Schedule I though it has now been approved for medical use

The legalization of marijuana is going through a rather complicated transitional phase, and there are also a few exceptions. The US Food and Drug Administration recently approved Epidiolex, which is used to treat rare conditions of epilepsy and contains CBD. The DEA has classified this as a Schedule 5 drug, indicating a low propensity for addiction and abuse.

The 2014 Farm Bill is often used by cannabis producers selling CBD products to legalize their activities. This law provides for the legal cultivation of cannabis if it is used for agricultural research or for another state pilot program. However, there is still some confusion as to whether the legalization of cultivation involves selling the crop or not. There is no clear definition of the legality of the CBD at the federal level. Therefore, it is a good idea to go through state laws to determine the legality of the CBD oil in a particular state.

Which States Allow Oil Production In The CBD?

Currently, CBD oil is fully legalized in Idaho, Nebraska, and South Dakota. Each state has its own specifications for the legal use of cannabis.

In ten states in the United States, the use of marijuana for medical and recreational purposes is fully legalized. The list of states includes Alaska, California, Maine, Colorado, Massachusetts, Oregon, Michigan, Washington, Vermont, and Nevada. If you are 18 or older, you can legally buy CBD oil at a pharmacy. Medical marijuana is approved in several other states, including Arizona, Florida, Connecticut, Arkansas, Illinois, Delaware, Hawaii, Missouri, New Jersey, Louisiana, New York, Minnesota, Montana, New Jersey, Maryland, North Dakota, Ohio, New Hampshire, Ohio, West Virginia, Rhode Island, Oklahoma, Utah, and Pennsylvania.

Cannabis is legal in about 33 states in one form or another. There are certain states in which the use of CBD oil is medically acceptable, and these are Alabama, Georgia, Indiana, Iowa, Kansas, Kentucky, Mississippi, North Carolina, South Carolina, Texas, Tennessee, Virginia, Wyoming, and Wisconsin.

Cannabis Cookbook

In 2018, the Senate introduced a new version of the law on farms to update the previous bill. An important part of this bill is that hemp will be legalized at the federal level if the bill is adopted. If and when hemp is legalized, this is a big step forward for the CBD industry, since CBD oil is extracted from hemp.

CHAPTER FOUR

BENEFITS OF CANNABIS

The use of marijuana for recreational purposes steadily grew from 1850- 1930. With the increase in the use of this drug, the government decided to classify cannabis as a Schedule I drug under the Controlled Substances Act of 1970. This led to an increase in the controversies that surrounded the medicinal benefits that cannabis offers. THC finally received the approval of the US Food and Drug Administration in 1985. The US government also sponsored a study in 1999 into the benefits of cannabis and how it helps certain conditions. This study was undertaken by the Institute of Medicine and showed that cannabis helps reduce the side effects brought about by chemotherapy. Since 1999, there have been various studies directed at proving the health benefits that cannabis offers. In fact, California was the first state to legalize the use of medical marijuana in 1966 and since then several states have legalized the use and distribution of medical marijuana.

In this section, you will learn about the various health benefits that cannabis offers.

Slows Down Cancer

A study that was published in the *Journal of Molecular Cancer Therapeutics* claimed that cannabidiol from cannabis is capable of stopping the spread of cancer by disabling a gene known as Id-1. In 2007, the researchers at the California Pacific Medical Center, San Francisco, discovered that CBD could also assist in preventing the cancer cells from spreading. The study that led them to this conclusion was based on experiments on breast cancer cells that have a rather high level of Id-1 and the researchers treated this with cannabidiol. This study showed optimistic results since the addition of CBD helped decrease the mutation of the Id-1 and also slowed the growth of the cancerous cells. Now it is believed that cannabis can help slow the growth of tumors in the brain, breasts, and even lungs.

Prevention of Alzheimer's

In a study[1] that was conducted by Kim Janda from the Scripps Research Institute in 2006, it was observed that THC could help to slow the progress of Alzheimer's. In this study, it was discovered that THC could help to slow the development of amyloid plaques by preventing the enzyme present in the brain, which synthesizes them. This harmful plaque tends to destroy brain cells and increases the risk of Alzheimer's. Controlling the development of these plaque cells helps prevent Alzheimer's.

Treating Glaucoma

Cannabis can be used in the treatment of glaucoma. Glaucoma is a severe problem where there is an increase in the pressure in the eye that can lead to the loss of vision and severe damage to the optic nerves. Several studies undertaken by the National Eye Institute have showed that cannabis can help to reduce the pressure within the eye and this, in turn, can help in the treatment of glaucoma.

---

[1] News Release | Scripps Research. (2019). Retrieved from https://www.scripps.edu/news-and-events/press-room/2006/080906.html

Reducing Arthritis

A study that was conducted in 2011 showed that cannabis could be used for reducing pain and inflammation that is associated with arthritis. The study also showed that it could help those suffering from rheumatoid arthritis get better sleep while reducing the pain and discomfort that they might experience due to their painful condition. The researchers present in various rheumatological departments in different hospitals started administering Sativex (a pain killer based on CBD) to their patients and within two weeks, the users of Sativex reported a reduction in their pain and an improvement in their ability to sleep.

Epileptic Seizures

A study conducted in 2003 showed that cannabis could help to control epileptic seizures. Robert J DeLorenzo, at the Virginia Commonwealth University, administered cannabis extracts as well as synthetic cannabis to epileptic rats and this helped in stopping seizures in the test subjects within ten hours. Further research suggests that THC can help to control seizures by stabilizing those brain cells that influence the excitability and regulate relaxation

Cannabis can help reduce certain neurological effects as well as the muscle spasms that painful conditions like multiple sclerosis can cause. A study published by the Canadian Medical Association showed that cannabis could be helpful in easing the pain that multiple sclerosis causes. In a clinical study that was conducted by Jody Cory Bloom, it was shown that cannabis could help significantly reduce the pain that these patients experience. The study consisted of 30 patients suffering from multiple sclerosis who weren't responding to any other pharmaceutical drugs. It was observed that by smoking cannabis for a couple of days, the pain that these individuals experienced was reduced. The THC present in cannabis binds itself with certain receptors present in nerves and muscles and this, in turn, helps to alleviate pain.

Soothing Tremors

Several studies conducted in Israel showed that the consumption of cannabis helps to reduce pain as well as the tremors associated with Parkinson's disease. In fact, it was also observed that cannabis improves the quality of sleep in those suffering from Parkinson's. Another notable discovery of this study was that the consumption of cannabis also helped in improving the motor skills among the patients who were a part of the study. Israel has legalized medical marijuana and a lot of continuous research is being conducted about the benefits of cannabis with the backing of the Israeli government

Crohn's Disease

Crohn's disease is a condition wherein an individual suffers from severe inflammatory bowel disorder accompanied by severe pain, diarrhea, nausea, vomiting, weight loss, and other troublesome symptoms. In a study that was conducted, it was discovered that the ingestion of cannabis via smoking helps to reduce the symptoms of Crohn's disease in the participants of the study. This was a rather small study, but a lot of researchers seem to agree that cannabis is an effective pain killer or suppressor and it can be quite helpful to those who suffer from painful conditions like Crohn's disease, multiple sclerosis, and so on. The cannabinoids from marijuana help to regulate the bacteria present in the gut and improve the function of the intestines. All this, in turn, helps to alleviate the painful symptoms associated with Crohn's disease.

Dravet's Syndrome

Dravet's Syndrome is a condition wherein a person suffers from seizures as well as developmental delays. Research was conducted on children suffering from Dravet's Syndrome who were offered medical marijuana with a high CBD and low THC content. According to this research, medical marijuana helped in reducing the seizures experienced by the participants.

Quitting Smoking and Drug Withdrawal

There is some evidence that is rather promising which shows that CBD present in cannabis can come in handy when people are trying to quit smoking. A pilot study showed that smokers who used an inhaler that had CBD present in it smoked fewer cigarettes than the ones who did not. Not just that, but CBD was also shown to help reduce nicotine addiction. Another similar study showed that CBD is quite helpful in reducing the symptoms of drug withdrawal. Researchers are of the opinion that some of the symptoms experienced by substance abuse users can be significantly reduced with the help of CBD. The symptoms that CBD helps rectify are anxiety, mood swings, pain, and insomnia. So, CBD can be used in reducing or even eliminating the symptoms of withdrawal.

Anxiety Disorders

Patients with chronic anxiety are often advised against consuming cannabis since the THC present in it can trigger or even amplify the paranoia that they might experience. However, a review presented in *Neurotherapeutics* suggests that while THC might amplify anxiety, CBD can help to reduce anxiety experienced by individuals suffering from any anxiety disorders. The research showed that CBD can help to reduce anxiety by calming the mind.

Reduces the Side Effects of Hepatitis C

The treatments available for Hepatitis C tend to produce rather severe side effects. In fact, the side effects can be so severe that at times patients aren't able to go through with their treatment. The common side effects include loss of appetite nausea, extreme fatigue, muscle pain, and even depression. However, by including cannabis as part of the treatment, the severity of these symptoms can be alleviated. In 2006, a study was published in the *European Journal of Gastroenterology and Hepatology* in which it was observed that over 80 percent of patients using cannabis were able to complete their treatment for Hepatitis C when compared to the existing rate of around 25 percent non-users of cannabis completing the necessary treatment. Cannabis also helps to improve the efficiency of Hepatitis C treatment.

Reducing the Side Effects of Chemotherapy

One of the most popular uses of medicinal marijuana is in combating the side effects of chemotherapy. Chemotherapy is the only means of slowing down or eliminating the growth of cancerous cells in the body. However, chemotherapy can take a toll on the health of the individual undergoing this therapy. The side effects of chemotherapy include extreme pain, severe nausea, and vomiting along with a loss of appetite. All these side effects can cause other health complications. Cannabis helps to reduce these side effects. As mentioned earlier, it is an effective means of reducing pain and nausea. Also, one of the effects of consuming cannabis is that it causes an increase in appetite, and this certainly comes in handy while treating chemotherapy patients

Acne

A study that was published by the *Journal of Clinical Investigation* and the National Institute of Health found that cannabis could be used to treat acne. Researchers used cannabis on the sebaceous glands and concluded that the chemical compound acts as an anti-inflammatory.

Diabetes

Diabetes develops in both people and animals. In a study conducted, cannabis was used on non-obese diabetic mice to see if it helped prevent the development of diabetes. There was no direct effect of cannabis on glucose levels; however, the treatment prevented the production of IL-12. It is essential to prevent this cytokine from being produced since it plays a huge role in the development of many autoimmune diseases.

Fibromyalgia

Opioid pain medications, corticosteroids, and anti-inflammatory medications are the most common methods used for treating fibromyalgia. A study conducted in 2011 focused on the effect of cannabis on patients who have fibromyalgia. The study showed promising results, which made way for the use of cannabis in future treatments. Fifty percent of the patients were subjected to cannabis treatment while the remaining 50 percent were subjected to traditional treatment. Those using cannabis showed significant improvement when compared to patients using traditional medication.

Cannabis can help treat a host of health problems. However, not many are comfortable with the idea of smoking cannabis. You no longer have to smoke cannabis to enjoy the benefits it offers! By using the simple recipes discussed in this book, you can reap all the benefits it offers without having to smoke it.

CHAPTER FIVE

SIDE EFFECTS OF CANNABIS

Now that you are aware of the various health benefits cannabis offers, in this section, you will learn about the different side effects the consumption of cannabis edibles can have on the body.

The effects that a cannabis user will experience depend on different factors like the dosage, the method with which cannabis is administered, any prior experience, level of tolerance, other drug use, personal expectations, state of mind, and the immediate environment as well as the individual's mood.

The short-term side effects of cannabis might or might not be experienced by all users. The consumption of cannabis can alter an individual's state of consciousness, as the user might experience a euphoric high and feel relaxed. It can also lead to the distortion of one's perception of space and time. The user might experience a sudden sensitivity to things around them and might even be able to experience things in a different manner. It can slightly alter an individual's primary senses like sight, taste, hearing, and smell. Other side effects include a spike in heart rate, bloodshot eyes, dilation of pupils, and an increase in appetite. Consumption of cannabis can also impair one's ability to concentrate and can inhibit the coordination between the body and the mind. Other negative side effects include anxiety, paranoia, panic, and self-consciousness.

A heavy dose of cannabis can lead to sedation, disorientation, and even toxic psychosis. It can also lead to severe mood swings, panic attacks and hallucinations. Therefore, it is always important that you calculate the right dosage before consuming cannabis. Start with a small dosage and you can gradually increase it until you find something that works for you.

The physical effects of cannabis can be experienced within a couple of minutes of its consumption. However, it can take anywhere between 10 to 30 minutes for it to be fully active, and these effects can last a couple of hours. THC is soluble in water, so it can also be stored by the fat cells within the body for a couple of months.

Apart from the short-term effects, consumption of cannabis can also have long-term effects. If the method of administration of cannabis is via smoking, then it can cause irritation of the lungs and increase the risk of contracting chronic bronchitis. Chronic use of cannabis can also lead to drug dependency. It can lead to a decrease in levels of concentration and the ability to remember things. Some people also experience a reduction in sex drive due to the constant and prolonged use of cannabis. Cannabis is a great way to deal with a lot of health conditions, but it is a good idea to consult your medical practitioner before you start using cannabis in any form.

There are a few things that you must absolutely avoid after administering cannabis. As mentioned earlier, it can lead to poor coordination. Therefore, please don't drive, operate any heavy machinery, or undertake the performance of hazardous activities after consuming cannabis. Cannabis can also lead to drowsiness and dizziness. Never consume any alcohol while using cannabis since this combination can lead to a severe loss of judgment and increase drowsiness or dizziness. Women must not use cannabis if they are pregnant, trying to become pregnant, or might become pregnant. The use of cannabis at the time of conception can increase the risk of birth defects. Also, women who are breastfeeding must not consume cannabis.

Cannabis Cookbook

CHAPTER SIX

CALCULATING THC DOSAGE

If you want to cook edibles, then you need to learn to calculate the THC dosage. In fact, this is one topic that no home cook can afford to skip. If the THC dosage in the edibles is too high or low, you will not experience any of the benefits that are associated with cannabis edibles. For calculating the dosage, you must consider a couple of factors like the strength of the cannabis and your tolerance toward it. The ideal dosage is usually around 10 to 15 milligrams. However, when it comes to edibles, it is always a good idea to be aware of the THC content per serving. There is a simple formula that you can use to determine the THC content, regardless of whether the plant matter you are using has been tested in a lab or not. That said, please keep in mind that this isn't a foolproof formula and it will only help you figure out the THC or the CBD content per serving of the cannabis edibles you cook. So, read on to learn about this formula and the way in which you can use it.

A lot of people aren't aware of the THC content in the plant material that they use. The usual average of THC in cannabis is around 10 percent. The simple formula that you must keep in mind is:

One gram of cannabis = 1000 milligrams and THC content is 10 percent of 1,000 milligrams. So, one gram of cannabis contains about 100 milligrams of THC. Now, by using this number, you must calculate the quantity of THC that's present in the cannabutter or cannabis-infused oil you plan to use. For instance, let us assume that the recipe calls for an ounce (around 28 grams) of cannabis for making a cup of cannabutter. An ounce of cannabis contains about 2800 milligrams of THC. The THC content or potency of the recipe will depend on the amount of cannabutter or oil the recipe calls for. If you are baking one batch of cookies (36 cookies), then you need to use about half a cup of cannabutter and this means that the total THC content of the batch of cookies is 1400 milligrams. Now that you know the total THC content, you can easily calculate the THC per cookie by dividing the total THC by the number of cookies baked. So, in this scenario, the THC content per cookie is 1400 milligrams/36 cookies = 38.8 milligrams per cookie.

Estimate the THC content in the plant material you are using and then divide it by 100 to obtain the THC content of the cannabis per milligram. Once you have this number, calculate the THC content in the infusion you are using and the amount of cannabis-infused oil or butter that the recipe calls for. Finally, divide this by the number of servings you can make with the recipe in order to obtain the appropriate dosage. If you feel that the dosage of THC as suggested by the recipe is too high, then you can reduce the amount of cannabis oil or butter you plan on using. Similarly, if the dosage isn't sufficient, then you merely need to increase the amount of cannabis oil or butter you are using.

The chart in this section provides the THC content that's necessary for experiencing a mild to strong psychotropic cannabis effect. The numbers given in the chart are based on hashish and cannabis grown indoors. A variety that's grown indoor typically has THC content between eight to 16 percent. Varieties grown outdoors have a THC content anywhere between four to eight percent. An individual will need about 20 to 30 milligrams of THC per kilogram of body weight for experiencing a mild psychotropic effect of cannabis. For instance, if an individual's weight is around 50 kg (110 pounds), then the quantity of THC that's necessary for a mild psychotropic effect is between 10 to 15 milligrams. If you weigh more, then you must adjust the THC dosage accordingly. If you are just getting started, then I suggest that you follow the numbers given in the following chart.

Body Weight	Mild Effect	Medium - Strong Effect
110 pounds	0.013 to 0.019 g	0.026 to 0.038g
130 pounds	0.015 to 0.022g	0.030 g to 0.044g
155 pounds	0.018 to 0.027g	0.036 to 0.054g
175 pounds	0.020 to 0.030 g	0.020 to 0.030 g

NOTE: If you are just getting started with cannabis, it is best if you start out with a small dosage. Everyone reacts differently to different dosages. Like with any new product, you will need to see how your body reacts to it. Depending on that reaction, you can determine whether you want to increase or decrease the dosage. The right dosage of cannabis will vary from one person to another. As a rule of thumb, a bigger person might need a higher dosage of cannabis than a smaller person. With cannabis, you have the freedom to increase the dosage by a few milligrams at a time for meeting your personal needs. If you have any preexisting medical conditions, then you must always consult a health-care professional before taking cannabis. A doctor or a medical professional can tell you take cannabis and the dosage you need to get the most out of it. So always consult your doctor first.

CHAPTER SEVEN

INTRODUCTION TO DECARBOXYLATION

About Decarboxylation

If you are interested in consuming cannabis edibles, then you can either purchase the prepackaged stuff or make the edibles at home. The cannabis edibles available on the market are quite expensive and tend to have varying contents of THC. If you decide to make cannabis edibles at home, you will have absolute control over the quality of ingredients you use.

Have you ever come across any scenes in a movie where someone ends up eating raw marijuana to prevent getting caught? Their eyes tend to go wide, and a lot of dramatic gasping follows suit. Here's a spoiler alert: no such thing happens when you consume raw cannabis. Why doesn't anything as dramatic as what's shown in movies happen when you eat raw cannabis? The answer to this is a process known as decarboxylation. This is essential if you want to enjoy the psychoactive effect of cannabis. Cannabinoids that are present within the trichomes present in raw cannabis flowers contain an additional carboxyl ring that's known as COOH. For instance, THCA (tetrahydrocannabinolic acid) is synthesized by the plant within the trichomes present in cannabis flowers. The cannabis that's distributed through dispensaries tends to contain labels about plant materials' cannabinoid content. THCA usually accounts for a major portion of the cannabinoid present in cannabis products that haven't been decarboxylated. THCA has different benefits, but it isn't a psychoactive ingredient, and only after decarboxylation will it be transformed into THC, the ingredient responsible for the psychoactive benefits of cannabis.

Time and heat are the primary catalysts needed for decarboxylation. Partial decarboxylation takes place when you dry and cure cannabis for a long time. This is the reason why some cannabis can test positive for trace amounts of THC along with THCA. Smoking and vaporizing are two means through which decarboxylation instantly takes place.

Decarboxylated cannabinoids in a vaporized form can be readily absorbed by the lungs, but when it comes to edibles, the cannabinoids present take longer for our bodies to absorb. Heating the cannabinoids steadily at a low temperature allows decarboxylation to take place and activates the THC present. Once the THC is activated, then you can easily infuse the cannabis with other ingredients to cook edibles.

Steps for Decarboxylating Cannabis at Home

Here are some simple steps that you can follow for decarboxylating cannabis at home.

- Preheat the oven for 20 minutes at 225°F. Doing this helps remove any moisture from the oven.

- Line an oven-safe dish with parchment paper.

- Crush the buds by breaking them into smaller pieces and by getting rid of any unnecessary plant materials like seeds. Place the crushed buds on the parchment paper. Ensure that the buds aren't crowded and are evenly arranged on the paper.

Cannabis Cookbook

- Place the plant material in the oven and allow it to bake at 250°F for about 25 minutes. The color of the cannabis will change from green to a shade of light brown.

- Once it has reached a light brown color, bake it for another 20 minutes or so, until the cannabis is medium brown in color. Keep checking on the cannabis every 10 minutes to ensure that it isn't burning.

- Remove the cannabis from the parchment paper and allow it to cool for a while. The cannabis will be quite crumbly and if you aren't careful while handling it, you will be left with powdered cannabis.

- Once it has cooled down, you can roughly grind it using a mortar and pestle. I prefer using a mortar and pestle or a manual weed crusher instead of a food processor. You need coarse flakes of cannabis, almost like oregano seasoning.

- Store the decarboxylated cannabis in an airtight container and keep it in a dry and dark place.

Please note that the decarboxylation process gives off a rather pungent herbal odor, so ensure that you turn on the exhaust fan in the kitchen!

CHAPTER EIGHT

COOKING WITH CANNABIS

In this section, you will learn about cooking with cannabis.

Cannabis Can Taste Good

If you aren't a fan of the woody and earthy aroma of cannabis, then you don't have to worry about it while cooking with cannabis. When you cook edibles, the original taste of cannabis will be overpowered by that of any other ingredient you use, such as chocolate or any other flavoring. Infusing cannabis with coconut oil, butter, or any other oil of your choice will give the oil or fat a rather nutty profile that perfectly complements any earthy spices like cinnamon, nutmeg, garlic, or any other spices that you can think of. Since the flavor of the bud is fully masked by any other flavorful ingredient you use, the edibles will not have any traces of the smell or flavor of weed. Once you infuse any oil or butter with cannabis, then you can start using that cannabis-infused butter for cooking savory dishes as well as desserts.

Not Limited to Heavy Foods

When you think of cannabis edibles, what is the first thing that pops into your head? Perhaps a cannabis-infused brownie? Who doesn't like a brownie? Just because you want to cook with cannabis, you don't have to use a lot of sugar or unnecessary calories. Most edibles that are readily available these days are full of processed sugars and carbs. However, please understand that edibles don't have to be calorie-dense foods. Cannabis is quite a versatile ingredient and can be easily incorporated into any recipe. The slightly citrusy and herbal notes in marijuana are quite similar to the ones present in spices like pepper, mint, or rosemary. Therefore, it can be used in a similar fashion. All these flavors work well together, and they don't necessarily have to be used to cook calorie-rich foods. You can use cannabis-infused butter or oil to cook pretty much anything you want. You can use cannabis-infused olive oil as a dressing for salads!

Select the Right Strain

The strain of marijuana that you use will determine the effect the edibles will have on you. For instance, a cannabis strain like Hindu Kush will have a rather drowsy effect and you will experience the same effect if you cook using that strain. Any of the uplifting strains of sativa also tend to have the same effect. You must not forget all these things before you start cooking with it. For instance, if you want a boost of energy in the morning, then you can add a drop or two of cannabis-infused coconut oil to your cup of coffee. If you opt for an OG strain, you will make yourself quite drowsy. So, you need to opt for a strain that has an uplifting effect!

You can Combine it with Alcohol

THC can be infused with alcohol and not just fats. Infusing cannabis with liquor is quite similar to infusing any liquor with herbs. Take some crushed marijuana, add it to a bottle of whiskey, seal it tightly, and leave it undisturbed in a dark place for a couple of weeks! Once the weed is infused with the liquor, you can use the infused liquor to make delicious cocktails! However, you must keep in mind that the potency of liquor increases when you infuse it with marijuana.

You can infuse cannabis with either fat or an oil-based ingredient if you want to cook with it. The list of fats that you can use include butter, lard, ghee, shortening, and any other nut or vegetable oil. If the recipe you decide to use does not contain any fatty ingredients, then you can use any spirit (cognac, vodka, rum, and so on) to dilute the cannabis concentrate. Any water-based alcohol like wine or beer is not a good carrier for cannabis oil. You can use cannabis oil in sweet and savory recipes alike. Make sure that you measure the sweetening or the spice flavors in the recipe to reduce the natural bitterness of cannabis oil.

Include it in Your Meal

Try to think of the different ways in which you can incorporate cooking with marijuana into your regular meals. You can even incorporate it into different social activities like dinner parties. For instance, food that's infused with cannabis can be a wonderful culinary experience. It not only increases one's appetite, but it also allows people to thoroughly enjoy their food and creates a rather intense experience. You can serve a simple appetizer infused with some cannabis and it will enable your guests to enjoy the entrée with some extra relish.

Prepare it Beforehand

A common mistake that a lot of newbies cooking edibles make is that they mix cannabis with butter and add it to a saucepan before they cook. Well, this is a terrible idea for two reasons. The first reason is that doing this prevents you from capturing a significant portion of the active agent present in cannabis and the second reason is that you can easily burn the useful substances present in cannabis. If you want to make edibles, then you need to plan ahead and make butter or oil infused with cannabis well before you start cooking. Infusing cannabis with oil or butter is a slow process that must not be rushed. To protect THC or the active ingredient present in cannabis, you must let it simmer on extremely low heat for a long time or even use a water bath. Exposing THC to direct heat will burn it, and the infused oil or butter will not be potent.

Try Doing it Yourself

If you have never tried cannabis edibles before or are planning on eating edibles that you purchased, then please don't consume them on an empty stomach. Readymade cannabis edibles tend to be rather unpredictable and consuming them on an empty stomach can overwhelm your system. Therefore, if you are interested in consuming edibles, then the best thing that you can do is to start cooking them at home! By making edibles at home, you will have absolute control over the quality and quantity of ingredients that you use.

Tips for Troubleshooting

Now that you are aware of different things that you must keep in mind while buying cannabis, there are some mistakes that you must avoid while cooking with cannabis. In this section, you will learn about different tips that will come in handy while cooking with cannabis.

Don't grind it too much

Most of the recipes that you find online for edibles recommend finely grinding cannabis for making cannabis-infused oils or butter. In fact, some of the commercially manufactured electronic appliances used for making cannabutter come with an inbuilt grinder. This doesn't make any sense to me. If you want to cook edibles without compromising their taste or potency, then I suggest that you don't grind the plant material into a fine powder. The resin-like trichomes you are trying to extract are present on the buds and the leaves of the cannabis plant and not within. So, if you grind cannabis into a fine powder, then you will end up adding a lot more of the plant material into the edibles instead of just the useful trichomes. All this will give the edibles a rather pungent and herby flavor, along with a green hue to the finished product. If you don't want the edibles to be unappetizing, then please don't grind the plant material into a fine powder.

Add water while infusing cannabis

A common mistake that a lot of people make is that they don't add any water while making cannabutter or cannabis-infused oil. I think it is a good idea to add some water to the cannabis and butter or oil mixture, especially if you want to cook it on the stovetop. Water enables you to infuse cannabis at a low temperature and it also prevents the cannabis from burning. If the plant material burns or gets scorched, then the active ingredient—the THC present in it—will be lost and it lends a rather unappetizing flavor to the edibles. If the active ingredient is lost, then the cannabis-infused oil or butter will not have any potency. Also, by adding water, you can eliminate some of the green color and herby flavor of cannabis. There is no hard and fast rule about the amount of water that you need to add, but I personally suggest adding water and butter or oil in equal proportions (a 1:1 ratio is ideal).

Cooking at a high temperature

As a rule of thumb, it is always advisable to cook cannabis at low temperatures. The THC tends to completely disintegrate if the cooking temperature exceeds 390°F. In fact, THC starts to disintegrate well before that. The temperature at which water starts to boil is around 212°F, so it is a good idea to add water while cooking with cannabis. Also, if you are cooking with infused oils or butter or any other marijuana concentrates, you need to keep an eye on the temperature. Never directly use cannabis-infused oils or butter while sautéing or frying anything. You must not expose cannabis-infused oils or butter to direct heat. You can add them to the batter and then cook the batter. Ensure that the oven temperature doesn't exceed 375°F. At this temperature, the food cooks, but THC doesn't disintegrate.

Always decarb cannabis

Excess heat will destroy THC in cannabis, but you need some heat to activate it. A lot of people fail to realize that raw marijuana plant material barely contains any THC. It contains THC acid and then you need to convert this THC acid into THC by a process known as decarboxylation. Take a moment to think about it; even if you want to smoke cannabis, you need to light the joint! The heat helps activate THC and without the heat, this chemical will stay inactive. When you infuse butter or oil with cannabis, then a portion of the decarb process is taken care of while infusing cannabis into the fat you desire. However, if you want to increase the potency of THC in the plant material, then you need to decarb it first. Not just kief, but even hash must be decarboxylated before you cook with it to increase its potency!

Adding too much marijuana

The easiest way to ingest cannabis is by eating it. At times people tend to get impatient, start thinking that the edibles aren't working, and overeat. Well, by the time the THC kicks in, they realize that they probably ate more than desired. Overdosing on cannabis is hardly ever fatal, but it can certainly increase paranoia and disorientation. Getting the dosage right is quite important when it comes to edibles. In fact, I think it is a bit of an art since there are a lot of different things that you must consider while deciding the dosage. The effect that cannabis has differs from one person to another. For instance, a dosage that might not even have a physical effect on one person might make someone else extremely drowsy. Different things like a person's capacity and tolerance towards marijuana determine the effect the plant material has on their body. If you aren't familiar with cooking with any plant material, then I suggest that you try vaping or smoking beforehand to determine its potency. Please remember that cooking cannabis increase its potency. If the batch you cook is quite potent, then you simply need to regulate the portions you consume.

Adding too little

Adding too much or too little cannabis will not give you the desired effect. If the cannabis oil or butter that you make is not as potent as you hoped, then you can always tweak it. You simply need to slowly reheat the cannabis oil or butter and add some more decarboxylated kief or hash to that mixture. You might be tempted to add as little cannabis as possible since it is an expensive ingredient, but don't let this urge control you. If the oil or butter is too potent, then you merely need to use smaller quantities of it! However, cooking with cannabis-infused oil or butter that isn't potent will certainly yield disappointing results.

Cleanliness matters

This might sound like a rather obvious thing, but please ensure that the cooking station is clean to prevent any contamination. You don't want to find any bread crumbs or cat hair in the cannabis edibles you cook, do you? The cooking equipment and the cooking station must be clean. To prevent cross-contamination, I suggest that you use a different set of kitchen equipment for cooking cannabis.

Sweet and savory recipes

You can infuse cannabis either with fat or with an oil-based ingredient if you want to cook with it. The list of fats you can use includes butter, lard, ghee, shortening, and other nuts or vegetable oil. If your chosen recipe does not contain fat, you can dilute the hemp concentrate with any alcohol (brandy, vodka, rum, etc.). Aqueous alcohol, such as wine or beer, is not a good carrier for hemp oil. You can use cannabis oil in both sweet and spicy recipes. Be sure to measure the sweetness or spice of flavors in a recipe to reduce the natural bitterness of hemp oil.

Control heat

Cannabis extraction is reduced when exposed to direct heat. If you don't put cannabis-rich fat right on a hot frying pan or frying pan, that's fine. The fat or oil you use should be at the same temperature as tea or coffee (160 to 185). If you use hemp drenched in alcohol, you do not need to preheat the alcohol.

Choose wisely

Carefully select the concentrate and measure the active ingredient before you start cooking. Always start small. Then you can gradually increase the level of concentrate in the recipe. Until you understand your ideal dosage, it is advisable to use a small amount of cannabis extract.

Marijuana is commonly referred to as an illegal drug. But edible marijuana is usually a prescribed medicine. The edible leaf is used to cure and suppress a variety of diseases. The preferred means of taking marijuana is through smoking, but only a few people know that you can cook with cannabis. The cooking procedure might seem intimidating and requires a lot of patience. It's not as simple as grinding the leaves and adding the hash but has a few rules that you must follow. You will learn more about all this in the coming chapters in the book.

Cannabis Cookbook

CHAPTER NINE

CANNABIS-INFUSED BASIC RECIPES

How to Decarb Cannabis:

Place a sheet of parchment paper on a baking sheet. Spread cannabis all over the sheet.

Place it in a preheated oven at 220°F for 35-60 minutes. Remove from the oven. This is what you call decarboxylated or decarbed marijuana/cannabis. Use this procedure when decarbed cannabis is mentioned in any of the recipes in this book.

Always adjust the cannabis according to your personal needs*

Cannabis Tincture

Cooking time: NA

Ingredients:

- 2 ounces cannabis, finely ground, decarbed
- 2 quarts grain alcohol like Everclear

Method:

1 Sanitize a 2-quart glass jar or mason jar.

Cannabis Cookbook

2   Add marijuana to the jar.

3   Fill the jar with alcohol.

4   Fasten the lid and place in a cool, dark place. Shake the jar every couple of days. Repeat this process for 2-3 weeks.

5   Strain with a cheesecloth or a fine wire mesh strainer into a jar. Pour into dropper bottles. Place in the refrigerator or a cool place until use.

6   Use as directed by your doctor.

Cannabutter / Margarine

Cooking time: 45-50 minutes

Ingredients:

- 1/2 ounce cannabis buds, finely ground
- 1 cup butter/margarine/vegan butter

Method:

1. Place a saucepan over low heat. Add butter or margarine. When the butter or margarine melts, add cannabis powder and stir frequently with a wooden spoon.

2. Let simmer for about 45-50 minutes. Turn off the heat.

3. Strain into a glass container that has a fitted lid. Press the residue with the back of a spoon. Discard the residue.

4. When the butter hardens, place in the refrigerator until use. If you want to make a larger quantity of butter, cook for 60-70 minutes. After the butter hardens, pour some water into the container to cover the butter. This way it lasts longer.

Cannabis-Infused Cooking Oil

Cooking time: 3 hours

Ingredients:

- 32 ounces cooking oil like olive oil or avocado oil or canola oil
- 1/2 ounce cannabis, decarbed

Method:

1. Place a saucepan over low heat. Add oil and warm.
2. Stir in the cannabis.
3. Cook for about 3 hours, stirring every 30 minutes. Don't let the oil simmer or boil.
4. Place cheesecloth over a fine wire mesh strainer, placed on a large heatproof bowl.
5. Strain the oil in a bowl using cheesecloth. Squeeze the cheesecloth to remove as much oil as possible.
6. Let the oil come to room temperature. Pour into an airtight container and use as required.

Canna-Flour

Cooking time: NA

Ingredients

- 2 cups all-purpose flour
- 1/2 ounce cannabis, decarbed, finely ground

Method:

1. Add flour and cannabis to a mixing bowl. Whisk until well incorporated either with a spatula or electric hand mixer with a whisk attachment.

2. Transfer to an airtight container. Place in a cool and dry place until use. It can last for 3 months.

Cannabis Cookbook

Cannabis Milk

Cooking time: 1 hour

Ingredients

- Water, as required
- 5 cups milk (use 2 1/2 cups per serving)
- 1/2 ounce marijuana leaves (use 1/4 ounce per serving)

Method:

1. Place a pot of water over low heat. Add marijuana leaves and simmer for 10-12 minutes.

2. Turn off the heat and drain the water. Keep the marijuana leaves in the pot.

3. Add milk and simmer on low heat for about 35-40 minutes. Stir frequently.

4. Simmer until the milk is reduced to nearly half its original quantity.

5. Strain through a fine wire mesh strainer placed over a bowl.

6. Serve hot or chill and serve later.

Marijuana Honey

Cooking time: 4 hours

Ingredients

- pounds honey

- 1/2 ounce marijuana (half of the sugar shack and half the bud) discard stems, crushed

Method

1. Take a large piece of cheesecloth and fold in the center to make a double layer. Place the marijuana in it. Roll the cheesecloth. Seal the marijuana well. It shouldn't come out of the cloth. Fasten with string at the center and the sides.

2. Pour honey in a crockpot. Place the cheesecloth bag in it.

3. Cover and cook on lowest setting for 4 hours. Stir every hour. The color of the honey will have darkened by the end of 4 hours. Make sure that the honey does not boil. Keep it on a very low setting.

4. Let the honey remain in the crockpot overnight.

5. Heat the honey slightly if the honey is not pourable. Remove the cheesecloth bag and squeeze with your hands. Let the drippings drop into the honey. Stir well.

6. Pour into airtight containers. Store in a cool and dry place.

Weed Sugar

Cooking time: 1 hour

Ingredients:

- 0.2 ounce cannabis, decarbed
- 7 ounces granulated sugar
- 1 cup high-proof, unflavored alcohol like Everclear

Method:

1. Add cannabis to a glass jar. Pour alcohol in it. Fasten the lid and shake the jar well every 5 minutes, for 20 minutes.

2. Strain the alcohol by passing through cheesecloth. Squeeze the cheesecloth to remove as much alcohol as possible. Discard the cannabis.

3. Preheat oven to 200°F.

4. Mix together sugar and strained alcohol in a baking dish. Stir until sugar dissolves completely.

5. Bake at 200°F.

6. Stir the mixture every 10-12 minutes for an hour or until dry and the sugar crystalizes again.

7. Remove from the oven and cool completely.

8. Store in an airtight container.

Coconut Cannabis Oil

Cooking time: 4-24 hours

Ingredients:

- 10 cups distilled water
- 2 cups organic coconut oil
- 4 ounces cannabis, finely ground

Method:

1. Add coconut oil into a crockpot.
2. Set the crockpot on the lowest setting and melt the oil.
3. Stir in water and cannabis and mix until well incorporated.
4. Set the crockpot on high setting. Let the mixture heat for 1 hour. Stir often.
5. Change the crockpot setting to low. Let the mixture infuse for 4-24 hours. Stir after every 50-60 minutes.
6. Place cheesecloth over a fine wire mesh strainer, placed over a large heatproof bowl.
7. Strain the oil in the bowl using a cheesecloth. Squeeze the cheesecloth to remove as much oil as possible.
8. Let the oil come to room temperature. Pour into an airtight container and refrigerate for 8-9 hours.
9. The oil will have hardened by now. Drain off the water and use the oil as required.

Cannabis Mayonnaise

Cooking time: NA

Ingredients

- 2 eggs
- 2 teaspoons prepared yellow mustard
- 2 tablespoons lemon juice
- 1 1/2 cups cannabis-infused oil
- 1 teaspoon minced garlic
- Salt and pepper to taste

Method

1. Blend together eggs, lemon juice, mustard, garlic, salt, and pepper in a blender. Blend until smooth.

2. While the blender is running on low speed, pour the cannabis-infused oil in a thin stream until the mayonnaise is emulsified and thick.

3. Transfer to an airtight container and refrigerate until use.

Cannabis Peanut Butter

Cooking time: NA

Ingredients

- 3 teaspoons cannabis-infused extra-virgin olive oil
- 4 tablespoons peanut butter

Method

1. Add oil peanut butter to a jar or bowl.
2. Mix well with a spoon until smooth and creamy.

Canna-Cream Cheese

Cooking time: 30-40 minutes

Ingredients:

- 1/2 gallon whole milk
- 1/4 teaspoon salt
- 1/2 quart cultured buttermilk
- 1/2 ounce cannabis, finely ground

Method:

1. Add milk and buttermilk to a saucepan. Heat the saucepan on a medium flame. Stir occasionally until the temperature of the milk shows 170°F on a candy thermometer.
2. Let the mixture simmer between 170°F and 175°F for around 12-15 minutes. Turn the heat off when the milk mixture begins to separate into curds.
3. Place many layers of cheesecloth inside a strainer. Place the strainer on a bowl.
4. Pass the mixture through the strainer. Retain the curds and use the milk that is remaining in some other recipe or discard it.
5. Cool the curds completely in the strainer.
6. Transfer to a blender. Add salt and blend until smooth.
7. Transfer to an airtight container and chill until use. It can last for 3-4 days.

Marijuana Vinaigrette

Cooking time: NA

Ingredients:

- 1/2 teaspoon minced garlic
- 1 teaspoon fresh basil or oregano or ½ teaspoon basil or oregano
- 7-8 tablespoons cannabis-infused oil
- 1/2 tablespoon red onion or shallot, minced
- 2 tablespoons balsamic vinegar or any other vinegar of your choice
- Salt to taste
- Pepper to taste

Method:

1. Add salt, pepper, garlic, oregano or basil, onion, and vinegar into a blender and blend until it become smooth.
2. While the blender is running, pour cannabis-infused oil in a thin stream. Blend until the vinaigrette is slightly thick. If your vinaigrette is not thickening, add more oil until the desired thickness is achieved.
3. Transfer to a bowl or jar. Add salt and pepper to taste.
4. Use in salads.

CHAPTER TEN

MUNCHIES

Sweet Potato Fries

Serves: 2-3

Cooking time: 20-30 minutes

Ingredients:

- 1 pound sweet potatoes (the orange variety), peeled if desired
- Sea salt to taste
- 1 small clove garlic, finely minced
- 1 tablespoon cannabis-infused extra-virgin olive oil
- 1 tablespoon flat leaf parsley, chopped
- 2 tablespoons parmesan cheese, grated

Method:

1. Preheat oven to 450°F.
2. Rinse the sweet potato pieces and dry by patting with kitchen or paper towels.

Cannabis Cookbook

3. Cut the sweet potatoes into fries.

4. Spread the sweet potatoes on a baking sheet.

5. Sprinkle salt and oil all over them. Toss well. Spread evenly all over the baking sheet, without overlapping.

6. Bake for 20 to 30 minutes.

7. Meanwhile, add garlic, parsley, and cheese into a bowl and stir.

8. When the fries are ready, transfer to the bowl of cheese and toss well.

9. Serve right away.

Weed Biscuits

Serves: 25-30

Cooking time: 12-15 minutes

Ingredients:

- 1 1/2 cups boiled, mashed sweet potatoes
- 2 tablespoons baking powder
- 3/4 cup cannabutter, unsalted, cold, cut into small cubes
- 1-2 cups milk
- 4 tablespoons sugar
- 2 teaspoons salt
- 3 cups all-purpose flour

Method:

1. Preheat oven to 425°F.
2. Add milk and sweet potatoes to a bowl and whisk well.
3. Mix together baking powder, sugar, salt, and flour in a bowl.
4. Add butter and mix using a fork or a pastry cutter until crumbly.
5. Mix the sweet potato batter and fold. If you find the mixture too very dry, then add some more milk.
6. Form into a smooth dough using your hands.
7. Roll the dough with a rolling pin. Chop into the desired shape

with a cookie cutter. Re-roll the scrap dough and cut out some more biscuits.

8. Gently lift the biscuits and place on a greased baking sheet, in a single layer. Bake in batches. Leave some gap between the biscuits.

9. Bake at 425°F for 12 to 15 minutes or until slightly hard and golden brown.

10. Remove from the oven and cool completely.

11. Transfer to an airtight container. Store at room temperature.

Cannabis Cookbook

Baked Apricot Brie

Serves: 20-25

Cooking time: 30-40 minutes

Ingredients:

- 2 brie rounds (8 ounces each)
- 2 cups cannabutter, melted
- 1/4 teaspoon salt
- 1 package filo dough sheets, thawed
- 2/3 cup apricot preserves or orange marmalade
- 1/2 cup roasted, salted, chopped almonds (optional)

Method:

1. Preheat oven to 375°F.
2. Cut the outer rind off the brie. You can use it in some other recipe if desired or discard it. Set aside.
3. Add cannabutter into a saucepan. Place over low heat until it melts. Turn off the heat.
4. Unfold the filo dough.
5. Pull out 2 filo sheets and place on your countertop, slightly overlapping at the edges. You should have a rectangle of approximately 24 x 17 inches.
6. Brush melted butter over the filo sheets.
7. Place 2 more filo sheets over this, again slightly overlapping at

the edges.

8. Repeat step 5-6. You should have at least 3 to 4 layers in all. The topmost layer should be brushed with butter.

9. Place one brie round in the center of the filo rectangle.

10. Smear 5-6 tablespoons of the apricot preserves over the brie.

11. Sprinkle salt and half the almonds.

12. Fold the edges of the filo layers over the brie, to cover it completely. Press the edges to seal.

13. Repeat steps 2 to 11 and make the other brie.

14. Place on a lined baking sheet, with the seam side facing down.

15. Bake for 30 to 40 minutes or until golden brown. You may find that the brie is coming out of the pressed edges.

16. Remove from the oven and let cool for 15 minutes.

17. Cut into slices and serve with crackers of your choice.

Cannabis Granola

Serves: 40-50

Cooking time: 30 minutes

Ingredients:

1. 1 cup marijuana-infused coconut oil
2. 2 cups chopped mixed nuts
3. 2 teaspoons baking soda
4. 3 teaspoons ground cinnamon
5. Flavoring of your choice like vanilla extract, strawberry extract, etc. (optional)
6. 1 cup brown flaxseed meal
7. 1 cup honey or maple syrup
8. 1/8 teaspoon salt
9. 6 cups oatmeal
10. 1 cup berries or fruits of your choice

Method:

1. Preheat oven to 300°F.
2. Line 2 large rimmed baking sheets with parchment paper. Add oatmeal, flaxseed meal, nuts, and cinnamon into a bowl and mix well.
3. If the oil is solid, then melt it either in a microwave or on the stovetop in a saucepan.

4. Whisk together oil, salt, honey, and any flavoring if using. Pour into the bowl of oatmeal mixture.

5. Mix until well incorporated. Transfer onto baking sheets. Spread evenly. Bake in batches.

6. Bake at 300°F for 20-30 minutes or until golden brown. Stir once, halfway through baking.

7. Remove the baking sheet from the oven and mix in the berries. Spread again on the baking sheet evenly.

8. Let cool slightly. Cut into bars. You can also make balls of the granola or any other shape of your choice.

9. Transfer to an airtight container and refrigerate until use.

Super Lemon Haze Mexican Guacamole

Serves: 8

Cooking Time: NA

Ingredients:

- 8 Hass avocados, peeled, pitted, mashed
- 4 small heads garlic, peeled, minced
- 2 cups small cherry tomatoes, finely chopped
- 2 sweet white onions, chopped
- Juice of 2 limes
- 2 ounces cannabis olive oil
- 2 teaspoons chili powder or to taste
- Cracked pepper to taste
- 2 teaspoons paprika or to taste
- 1 teaspoon cayenne pepper or to taste
- Sea salt to taste

Method:

1. Mix all the ingredients in a bowl and stir well until thoroughly combined.
2. Cover and chill for a while in order to allow the flavors to mingle.

3. Serve with vegetable sticks or crackers.

Stuffed Mini Peppers

Serves: 8 (4 pepper halves per serving)

Cooking time: 20 minutes

Ingredients:

- 16 mini peppers, split, deseeded
- 2 chorizo sausages, thinly sliced
- 2 teaspoons garlic, minced
- Salt to taste
- Pepper to taste
- 6-8 tablespoons cannabis-infused olive oil
- 10 scallions, sliced
- 3 cups fresh bread crumbs
- 4-6 tablespoons crumbled goat cheese
- 1-2 tablespoons olive oil, if required

Method:

1. Preheat oven to 300°F.
2. Line a large baking sheet with parchment paper.
3. Place pepper halves on it.

4. Place a pan over medium heat. Add oil and heat. When the oil is heated, add chorizo and cook for a few minutes. Remove the chorizo along with the cooked oil into a bowl. Set aside.

5. Place the pan back over medium heat.

6. Stir in the scallions into the pan. Cook for 2 to 3 minutes. Stir in garlic, salt, pepper, and bread crumbs. Mix well. Stir in some olive oil if the mixture is looking very dry.

7. Add chorizo along with the oil and mix well. Fill the pepper halves with this mixture. Press the filling well into the peppers.

8. Place some goat cheese on top of each pepper.

9. Bake for 20-30 minutes until the cheese is golden brown.

Cannabis Cookbook

Monster Munchie Balls

Serves: 20-25

Cooking time: 8-10 minutes

Ingredients:

- 3/4 cup cannabutter
- 2 tablespoons chunky peanut butter
- 1 tablespoon cocoa powder or chocolate syrup
- 1 1/2 cups rolled oats or granola
- 1 1/2 tablespoons honey

Method:

1. Add cannabutter to a saucepan. Place saucepan over low heat. Add the remaining ingredients and stir constantly until well incorporated. Cook for a couple of minutes. Stir constantly.
2. Transfer to a baking dish. Cool slightly. Freeze for 10-12 minutes until semi-soft in consistency.
3. Scoop with an ice-cream scoop and place in an airtight container lined with wax paper.

Note: First-timers should not eat more than half a scoop.

Hialeah Hash Browns

Serves: 4-5

Cooking time: 15 minutes

Ingredients:

- 1 pound fresh malangas, peeled, chopped, or grated
- Hash-butter to fry
- 2 eggs
- Salt and pepper to taste
- 1/2 teaspoon garlic powder

Method:

1. Add eggs, malangas, salt, garlic, and pepper into a bowl and mix until well combined.
2. Chill for an hour.
3. Place a deep pan over medium flame. Add hash-butter and let heat. Make small balls of the mixture.
4. When the butter melts, add a few of the malanga balls and fry until they turn golden brown and crisp.
5. Remove and place on a plate.
6. Fry the rest in batches.
7. Serve with a dip of your choice.

CHAPTER ELEVEN

BREAKFAST RECIPES

Banana Nut Bread

Serves: 20-25

Cooking time: 60-90 minutes

Ingredients:

- 1 cup brown sugar
- 1 cup granulated sugar
- 2 eggs
- 2 teaspoons milk
- 2 teaspoons ground cinnamon
- 2 teaspoons baking powder
- 2 teaspoons baking soda
- 1 cup chocolate chips
- 1 cup cannabutter

- 6 bananas, peeled, mashed
- 1 cup walnuts, chopped
- 1 teaspoon vanilla extract
- 3 cups flour
- 1 cup whole-wheat flour
- 2 teaspoons baking powder

Method:

1. Preheat oven to 325°F.
2. Add cannabutter, brown sugar, and sugar to a mixing bowl and beat with an electric hand mixer until creamy.
3. Add eggs at a time and beat well each time.
4. Beat until the mixture is light and creamy. Set aside for a while.
5. Mix together whole-wheat flour, baking soda, baking powder, flour, and cinnamon in a bowl and set aside.
6. Add bananas, vanilla, and milk into a bowl and beat until well combined. Pour into the bowl of butter mixture.
7. Whisk until well combined.
8. Add the mixture of dry ingredients mixture into it and mix well.
9. Add the walnuts and chocolate chips and mix well.
10. Pour into a greased baking pan or large loaf pan.
11. Bake at 325°F for 1 to 1 1/2 hours or until brown on top.

12. Cool on your countertop for 15 minutes.

13. Invert onto a plate. Cool until warm.

14. Slice and serve.

Weed French Toast

Serves: 8 (2 toasts each)

Cooking time: 45 minutes

Ingredients:

- 8 eggs
- 16 slices, sliced crosswise, from French baguette
- 6 tablespoons cannabutter
- 3 tablespoons butter, unsalted, plus extra for greasing
- 1 1/2 cups milk
- 1 1/2 teaspoons vanilla extract
- 5 tablespoons maple syrup
- 1 1/2 cups milk
- 1/3 cup sugar
- 3/4 teaspoon salt
- Powdered sugar

Method:

1. Preheat oven to 350°F.
2. Grease the baking dish with butter.
3. Add both the butters to a bowl and mix well. Spread this mixture on one side of each slice of bread.

4. Lay the bread slices in the baking dish, buttered side facing up.

5. Whisk together the rest of the ingredients in a bowl until well combined.

6. Pour this mixture over the bread slices. Press down with a spoon.

7. Cover and chill overnight.

8. Bake for about 45 minutes or until it turns golden brown.

9. Remove from oven and cool for 5 minutes.

10. Sprinkle powdered sugar and serve.

Krispy Kreme Doughnuts

Serves: 20-25

Cooking time: 20-30 minutes

Ingredients:

For donuts:

- 6 tablespoons milk
- 2 teaspoons dry active yeast
- 6 tablespoons sugar
- 4 tablespoons butter, at room temperature
- Oil to fry, as required
- 6 tablespoons boiling water
- 3 cups all-purpose flour or more if required
- 2 eggs, slightly beaten
- 1/4 teaspoon salt

For glaze:

- 2/3 cup cannabutter
- 3 teaspoons vanilla extract
- 4 cups confectioners' sugar
- 8 tablespoons water, or as required

Method:

1. Add boiling water and milk into a large bowl. Stir in 1/2 tablespoon sugar and yeast. Set aside in a warm place for 10-15 minutes or until frothy.

2. Add flour, remaining sugar, and salt into a bowl and mix well. Add butter and cut into the mixture with pastry cutter or using your hands, until crumbly.

3. Stir in the eggs and yeast solution and stir until smooth dough is formed.

4. Dust your countertop with some flour. Place the dough on your countertop and knead the dough for 8-10 minutes until supple. Tiny bubbles should be visible on the underside.

5. Place the dough in the mixing bowl. Cover with cling wrap and let sit until it rises and is around twice its original size.

6. Divide the dough into 7-8 pieces. Pull each piece until it is about 1 to 1 1/2 inches width and a long log.

7. Cut into 1-inch pieces. Shape into donuts. Place on a baking sheet. Cover with some cloth and set aside. In a while, the donuts will rise.

8. Place a deep pan over medium heat. Pour enough oil to cover at least 3 inches of the pan. Let the oil heat.

9. When the temperature of the oil reaches 375°F, carefully lower a few donuts at a time into the oil. Fry until golden brown. Remove with a slotted spoon and place on a plate lined with paper towels.

10. Fry the remaining dough in batches.

Cannabis Cookbook

11. Meanwhile, add all the ingredients for glaze into a saucepan and place over medium heat. Stir frequently until sugar dissolves completely. Turn off the heat. Cool for 5-8 minutes.

12. Dip the donuts in the glaze and place on a wire rack or on a plate lined with paper towels.

13. If the glaze has turned cold, heat again until warm.

14. Serve warm or at room temperature.

Breakfast "Baked" Burritos

Serves: 2

Cooking time: 15 minutes

Ingredients:

- 2 eggs
- 2 flour tortillas (10 inches each)
- 1 1/2 ounces cheddar cheese, shredded
- 1 tablespoon cannabutter
- 3 ounces bacon, cut into strips
- 6-7 tablespoons refried beans

Method:

1. Place a large deep skillet over medium heat. Add the bacon and cook until crisp.
2. Remove on a plate lined with paper tissues so they soak the oil.
3. Wrap the tortillas in foil and heat in the oven.
4. Place a nonstick skillet over medium heat. Add cannabutter.
5. When the butter melts, crack and fry the eggs according to the way you like them cooked.
6. Place the warmed tortillas on your countertop.
7. Spread refried beans over the tortillas. Place a few strips of bacon and an egg on each tortilla.

8. Sprinkle cheese, roll, and serve.

Canna-Scrambler

Serves: 2

Cooking time: 15-17 minutes

Ingredients:

- 1 tablespoon cannabutter
- Salt to taste
- 4 eggs
- 1/2 cup milk
- Pepper to taste

Method:

1. Preheat oven to 350°F.
2. Add cannabutter to a baking dish.
3. Place the baking dish in oven for 5 minutes or until the butter melts.
4. Add salt, pepper, and eggs into a bowl. Whisk well. Add milk, a little at a time, and whisk well each time.
5. Transfer to the baking dish.
6. Bake in oven for 10 minutes.
7. Stir and bake until the eggs are cooked to the desired doneness.
8. Serve immediately.

Cannabis Breakfast Egg Cups

Serves: 6

Cooking time: 15-20 minutes

Ingredients:

- 6 sandwich bread slices
- 3/4 cup shredded cheddar cheese
- Pepper to taste
- Salt to taste
- 6 slices bacon, cooked, crumbled
- 2 tablespoons melted cannabutter
- 6 eggs
- 1 tablespoon minced fresh thyme
- Canna-oil, to grease

Method:

- Preheat oven to 375°F.
- Grease a six-count muffin pan with some canna-oil.
- Place bread slices on countertop. Roll with a rolling pin until flat.
- Cut each slice of bread into 2 equal triangles.
- Place 2 pieces of bread (triangles) in each cup on the bottom

Cannabis Cookbook

as well as the sides.

- Brush melted cannabutter over the slices.

- Bake at 375°F for 7-8 minutes.

- Divide the cheddar cheese among the muffin cups.

- Crack an egg into each cup. Sprinkle salt and pepper over it.

- Bake until the eggs are cooked to the desired doneness.

Cannabis Cookbook

Canna-Cheesy Egg Benedict

Serves: 8

Cooking time: 20 minutes

Ingredients:

- 2 tablespoons cannabutter
- 1 1/2 cups milk
- 2 tablespoons shredded parmesan cheese,
- 4 tablespoons shredded cheddar cheese
- 3 1/2 tablespoons all-purpose flour
- 1/2 teaspoon Dijon mustard
- Salt to taste
- White pepper to taste

<u>For the poached eggs</u>

- 1 teaspoon white vinegar
- 4 English muffins, split, toasted
- 8 strips bacon, cooked, crumbled
- 8 cold eggs
- 8 slices Canadian bacon, warmed

Method:

Cannabis Cookbook

1. To make cheese sauce: Place a saucepan over medium heat. Add cannabutter and melt. Add flour and stir for a few seconds.

2. Pour the milk slowly, stirring simultaneously. Simmer until the sauce becomes thick. Stir constantly all the while.

3. Lower the heat. Add cheese, salt, pepper, and Dijon mustard and continue mixing until the cheese starts melting.

4. Remove from heat. Cover and set aside.

5. Place a large deep skillet over medium heat. Pour enough water in to cover about 3 inches from the bottom of the skillet.

6. Add vinegar and bring to the boil.

7. Crack an egg into a cup. Slowly slide the egg into the boiling water.

8. Repeat the previous step with the remaining eggs (add only as many eggs that can fit in the skillet) cook the rest in batches.

9. Cook until the eggs are set.

10. Place a Canadian bacon slice over each of the muffin halves. Place a poached egg over the bacon.

11. Spoon some cheese sauce over it.

12. Finally, place the crumbled bacon over it and serve.

Denver Omelet

Serves: 4

Cooking time: 12-15 minutes

Ingredients:

- 6 large eggs
- 1 cup chopped red or green bell pepper
- 8 slices bacon
- 1 teaspoon salt or to taste
- 1 cup chopped onion
- 1 cup cooked diced ham
- 2 tablespoons cannabutter
- 1 teaspoon pepper or to taste

Method:

1. Place a skillet over low heat. Add butter and melt. When butter melts, add onion, ham, pepper, and bacon and cook for a few minutes until vegetables are tender.

2. Meanwhile, whisk eggs and season with salt and pepper.

3. Spread the meat and vegetables in the skillet. Pour the eggs into the skillet. Cook them until the underside is golden brown. Flip and cook until the other side is golden brown.

4. Carefully slide the omelet onto a plate. Cut into 4 wedges and serve.

Oatmeal Pancakes

Serves: 6-8

Cooking time: 20-30 minutes

Ingredients:

- 2 tablespoons ghee (clarified butter)
- 2 cups rolled oats
- 2 tablespoons nut butter
- 8-16 drops cannabis tincture
- 2 ripe bananas, peeled, sliced
- 2 large eggs
- 2 tablespoons honey

Method:

1. Add banana, eggs, oats, and tincture into a blender and blend until smooth.
2. Pour the batter into a bowl.
3. Place a skillet over medium heat. Add about 1/4 tablespoon ghee and let it melt.
4. Pour about 1/4 cup batter on the pan. Bubbles will appear on the pancake. Cook until golden brown on the bottom. Flip sides and cook until the other side turns golden brown. Remove the pancake from the pan.
5. Repeat steps 3-4 and make the remaining pancakes.

6. Serve with honey or nut butter or any other toppings of your choice.

Potffles (Medicated Waffles)

Serves: 5-6

Cooking time: 25-30 minutes

Ingredients:

- 1 egg
- 1 cup cannaflour
- 3 tablespoons melted cannabutter (or regular butter if desired)
- 1/2 teaspoon salt
- 2 teaspoons baking powder
- 1 teaspoon granulated sugar
- 3/4 cup warm milk

Method:

1. Add flour, salt, baking powder, and sugar to a bowl and stir until the mixture comes together.

2. Add egg in another bowl and whip lightly. Add milk and cannabutter and stir.

3. Pour this batter in the bowl of flour and beat well. The batter should not be very smooth. It should have a few lumps here and there.

4. Pour a ladle of batter into a preheated waffle iron. Cook until golden brown.

5. Repeat the previous step and make the remaining waffles.

Weed Bread

Serves: 25-30 slices

Cooking time: 40-50 minutes

Ingredients:

- 0.35 ounces marijuana flowers, deseeded, de-stemmed, ground coarsely
- Flaxseed meal or cornmeal for dusting
- 1/2 teaspoon active dry yeast
- 6 cups all-purpose flour or 4 cups flour and 2 cups whole-wheat flour
- 2 1/2 teaspoons salt
- 3 1/2 cups lukewarm water (110°F)

Method:

1. Add marijuana flowers, yeast, flour, and salt to a mixing bowl. Whisk until well combined. Add lukewarm water and mix to form sticky dough.

2. Cover the bowl with cling wrap and keep it in a warm place for 12-16 hours or until the dough doubles in size and tiny bubbles may be visible on the top of the dough.

3. Dust your countertop with flaxseed meal. Dust your hands as well.

4. Place the dough on your countertop. Fold the dough a few times to form into a ball. Place dough on a cotton cloth, with

its seam side facing down. Sprinkle some cornstarch on top of the dough.

5. Wrap the dough lightly with the cloth and set aside for 2 hours to rise.

6. Preheat the oven to 450°F. Place a large greased loaf pan or Dutch oven in the oven while preheating.

7. Transfer the dough into the heated loaf pan carefully with its seam side facing up.

8. Cover with a lid or aluminum foil and bake for 40-50 minutes.

9. Uncover and continue baking for another 8-10 minutes. This is done to get a crust on top.

10. Turn off the oven and let the bread remain in the oven for 5 minutes.

11. Remove the bread from the oven and cool on a wire rack completely.

12. Slice and serve.

Quinoa Corn Cannabis Muffins

Serves: 20-25

Cooking time: 45 minutes

Ingredients:

- 1 cup quinoa, rinsed
- 2 cups water
- 2 cups whole-wheat pastry flour or canna-flour
- 1/2 teaspoon salt
- 1 cup light brown sugar or low-carb sweetener of your choice
- 1/2 cup cannabutter, melted
- 2 teaspoons vanilla extract
- 1 cup grilled or cooked corn (use only the kernels)
- 2 cups quinoa flour
- 2 teaspoons baking soda
- 2 eggs
- 2 1/2 cups plain yogurt

Method:

1. Preheat oven to 350°F.
2. To cook quinoa: Place a saucepan over medium heat. Add quinoa and water and stir.

3. When it starts to boil, lower the heat and cover with a lid. Cook until dry.

4. Turn off the heat and fluff using a fork. Cover and set aside for some time.

5. Add flour, quinoa flour, salt, sugar and baking soda into a mixing bowl. Stir until well combined.

6. Add eggs, yogurt, butter and vanilla into another bowl and whisk well. Pour into the mixture of dry ingredients. Stir until well combined and free from lumps.

7. Grease 2 muffin tins of 12 counts each.

8. Pour batter into the muffin tins. Fill up to 3/4. Bake in batches if required.

9. Bake at 350°F for 25 minutes.

Breakfast Sandwiches

Serves: 4

Cooking time: 15 minutes

Ingredients:

- Salt to taste
- Pepper to taste
- 0.1-0.14 ounces cannabis, finely chopped
- 4 eggs, beaten
- 4 tablespoons butter
- 8 slices Velveeta cheese
- 8 slices bacon
- 8 slices bread

Method:

1. Place a nonstick skillet over low heat. Add bacon and cook until it becomes crisp. Remove with a slotted spoon and place on a plate that is lined with paper towels.
2. Whisk together eggs, salt, and pepper and pour the mixture in the skillet. Scramble and cook the eggs.
3. Butter the bread on one side only.
4. Take half the slices of bread. Sprinkle half the cannabis over them.

5. Place one cheese slice on each bread slice. Place a slice of bacon over the cheese. Divide and place the scrambled eggs over them.

6. Place another slice of bacon over the scrambled eggs.

7. Place another cheese slice over the bacon. Sprinkle the remaining cannabis

8. Cover with the other 4 slices of bread, with the buttered side facing down. Press the sandwiches.

9. Place the sandwiches in a microwave and microwave for a few seconds until the cheese melts.

10. Chop into desired shape and serve.

Note: You can replace cannabis and butter with cannabutter

Cannabis Coffee Cake

Serves: 30-35

Cooking time: 20-30 minutes

Ingredients:

- 3/4 cup sugar
- 4 1/2 cups flour
- 2 eggs
- 1 1/3 cups milk
- 3/4 cup vegetable shortening
- 2 packages active yeast
- 2 eggs
- 3 tablespoons cannabutter, melted
- 1/2 teaspoon salt

Method:

1. Preheat oven to 375°F.
2. Grease a large baking pan or 2 smaller baking pans with cooking spray or some oil. Set aside.
3. Add 2 cups flour and yeast into a bowl and stir.
4. Place a saucepan over medium heat. Add milk, 1/2 cup sugar, and vegetable shortening.
5. Stir a couple of times. Turn the heat off when vegetable

shortening becomes softer.

6. Transfer to the bowl of yeast and beat until well mixed.

7. Add eggs, one at a time, and beat well each time. Add remaining flour and mix until well combined. You will have malleable dough.

8. Transfer the dough to the baking pan. Scatter almonds on top. Sprinkle remaining sugar on top of the dough.

9. Cover the baking pan with a clean, moist cloth. Let it sit for around an hour. The dough should have risen by now.

10. Bake at 375°F for about 20 minutes.

11. Remove from the oven and cool.

12. Cut into slices and serve.

Café De Cannabis

Serves: 2

Cooking time: 5 minutes

Ingredients:

- 2 cups freshly brewed Cuban coffee
- 1/2 teaspoon ground cinnamon
- 2 good pinches Moroccan hash
- 2 tablespoons sugar
- 1/4 teaspoon ground nutmeg

Method:

1. Pour hot coffee into 2 cups.
2. Divide equally and add cinnamon, sugar, Moroccan hash, and nutmeg to the cups and stir.
3. Serve right away.

CHAPTER TWELVE

LUNCH RECIPES

Marijuana Avocado Shake

Serves: 1

Cooking Time: NA

Ingredients:

- 1/2 avocado, peeled, pitted, chopped
- Ice cubes, as required
- 1 1/2 tablespoons sugar or any other sweetener of your choice to taste
- 3/4 cup canna-milk

Method:

1. Add avocado, ice cubes, sugar, and canna-milk to a blender and blend well.
2. Pour into a tall glass and serve.

Banana and Strawberry Smoothie Infused with Cannabis

Ingredients:

- 1/4 cup orange juice
- 3/4 cup frozen strawberries
- 0.004 ounces hash oil or kief hash, decarbed
- 1/2 cup coconut milk
- 1 small banana, sliced, frozen
- 1/2 tablespoon hemp seeds (optional)

Method:

1. Add strawberries, kief hash, orange juice, banana, coconut milk, and hemp seeds (if using) to a blender.
2. Blend for 30-40 seconds or until smooth.
3. Pour into a tall glass and serve.

Cannabis Vegetable Tart

Serves: 4

Cooking time: 25 minutes

Ingredients:

- 1/2 frozen puff pastry sheet, thawed
- 1/2 leek, sliced
- 1 cup torn Swiss chard
- 1/4 teaspoon sweet paprika
- Salt to taste
- 3 tablespoons cannabutter
- 1/2 yellow bell pepper, chopped
- 2-4 tablespoons crumbled goat cheese
- 1/4 teaspoon cayenne pepper

Method:

1. Preheat oven to 350°F.
2. Take a baking sheet and place half a sheet of puff pastry over it.
3. Place a skillet over low heat. Add cannabutter. When butter melts, add leek and pepper and cook until slightly tender.
4. Stir in chard and cook for one minute. Turn the heat off.
5. Spoon the vegetables on the pastry sheet. Scatter goat cheese

on top.

6. Bake at 350°F for 10-12 minutes or until the crust turns brown.

Smoked Mac 'n' Cheese

Serves: 2

Cooking time: 40 minutes

Ingredients:

- 2 cups milk
- 1/4 cup unsalted butter
- 1/4 cup cold cannabutter
- 1/2 tablespoon melted cannabutter
- 1/2 cup flour
- Salt and pepper, to taste
- 1/8 teaspoon cayenne pepper or to taste
- 1/2 cup smoked mozzarella cheese, grated
- 1/2 cup parmesan cheese, grated and divided
- 1/2 cup cheddar cheese, shredded
- 1/2 cup shredded American or Swiss cheese
- 2 tablespoons bread crumbs

Method

1. Preheat oven to 400°F.
2. Place a skillet over low heat. Add butter and cold cannabutter. When butter melts, stir in the flour and cook for 2-3 minutes

until aromatic.

3. Meanwhile, heat milk. Turn off the heat when the milk is quite hot. Do not boil it.

4. Pour milk into the skillet, stirring constantly. Stir in the seasonings. Cook until thick, stirring all the while. When the mixture begins to boil, turn off the flame. Add pasta, smoked mozzarella, 6 tablespoons Parmesan, cheddar cheese, and American cheese. Mix well. Heat thoroughly and stir. Turn off the heat.

5. Transfer to a baking dish.

6. Bake at 400°F until the top is light brown.

7. Take out of the oven and cool for about 10 minutes and then serve.

Spinach Cannabis Quiche

Serves: 4

Cooking time: 30 minutes

Ingredients:

- 1/4 cup cannabutter
- 1/2 cup milk
- 1/2 small onion, finely chopped
- 2.25 ounces canned mushrooms, drained, chopped
- 4 ounces cheddar cheese, shredded
- Salt and pepper to taste
- 2 cloves garlic, finely minced
- 5 ounces frozen spinach, thawed, drained
- 3 ounces crumbled feta cheese
- 2 eggs, beaten
- 1 small (6 inch) deep pie crust, unbaked

Method:

1. Preheat oven to 400°F.
2. Place a skillet over low heat. Add cannabutter. When butter melts, add onion and garlic and sauté well.
3. Add mushroom and spinach and mix well. Cook for a couple

of minutes until spinach wilts.

4. Stir in feta cheese and half the cheddar cheese. Add salt and pepper to taste. Mix well. Cook until cheese melts. Turn off the flame.

5. Spread this mixture over the pie crust.

6. Whisk together eggs and milk in a bowl. Pour the filling over the crust.

7. Bake at 400°F for 15 minutes or until the top is light brown.

8. Remove from the oven. Cool for about 10 minutes and then serve.

Weed Ramen Noodles

Serves: 2

Cooking time: 15 minutes

Ingredients:

- 2 servings ramen kimchi noodles
- 4 tablespoons butter
- -0.14 ounces weed, ground
- Hot chili sauce, to taste
- 1/2 cup cheese, grated
- 4 cups water
- teaspoon dried oregano

Method:

1. Place a pot over medium heat. Add water and weed. Heat, but don't allow to boil.
2. Add butter and simmer until the weed turns slightly brown in color. Do not boil. If it starts boiling, remove from heat and set aside for a while. Place it again over heat until it turns slightly brown in color.
3. Add the ramen noodles, kimchi, flavoring packet that comes with it, hot sauce, oregano, and cheese.
4. Simmer until the noodles are cooked.
5. Ladle into soup bowls and serve.

Marijuana Meatloaf

Serves: 10-12

Cooking time: 45-60 minutes

Ingredients:

- 2 large eggs
- 1/2 ounce cannabis
- 2 pounds ground beef or lamb or pork
- 1 package crushed saltines
- 1 cup green bell pepper, chopped
- 1 cup onion, chopped
- 1 cup melted cannabutter or canna-oil
- 1 1/2 teaspoons black pepper, powdered
- 2 cloves garlic, minced
- 1 1/2 teaspoon salt

Method

1. Preheat oven to 350°F.
2. Add meat, garlic, onion, and bell pepper to a large bowl and knead well.
3. Stir in saltines, cannabutter, and cannabis.
4. Transfer to a greased loaf pan. Spread evenly with a spatula.

5. Bake at 350°F for about 45-60 minutes.

6. Remove the loaf pan from oven. Set aside for a while to cool slightly.

7. Slice and serve.

Raspberry Pear Grilled Cheese Sandwich

Serves: 4

Cooking time: 20 minutes

Ingredients:

- 8 slices hearty whole-grain bread
- 2 ripe pears, peeled, cored, thinly sliced
- 4 tablespoons cannabutter, at room temperature
- 7-8 tablespoons raspberry jam or preserves
- 8 slices Muenster cheese
- Salt to taste

Method:

1. Place a large skillet over medium-high heat.
2. Spread 1/2 tablespoon butter on one side of a slice of bread. Spread 1 1/2-2 tablespoons jam on the other side of the bread slice.
3. Place the bread slice on the skillet, buttered side facing down.
4. Place a few pear slices over the jam side of the bread (the top). Place 2 slices of cheese over the pears. Lower the heat to low heat.
5. Cover the pan with a lid. Cook for a couple of minutes until cheese melts.
6. Spread butter on another slice of bread. Cover this slice over

the sandwich, with the buttered side facing up.

7. Carefully lift the entire sandwich and flip sides. Cook until the underside is golden brown.

8. Remove to a plate. Cut into desired shape and serve.

9. Repeat steps 2-8 and make the remaining sandwiches.

Ham and Cheddar Panini

Serves: 4

Cooking time: 10 minutes

Ingredients:

- 4 rolls, split
- 1 pepper, cut into round slices
- 8 ounces ham, thinly sliced
- 2 tomatoes, thinly sliced
- 4 tablespoons canna-oil
- 8 ounces cheddar cheese, sliced
- Arugula leaves, as required
- 1 cup sauerkraut, drained

Method:

1. Place a skillet over low heat. Add oil and heat. Add pepper and cook until it becomes slightly tender. Take off the heat.
2. Place ham on the bottom half of the rolls. Divide the rest of the ingredients equally. Layer with arugula followed by tomatoes and cheese. Next layer with bell pepper slices and sauerkraut.
3. Cover with the top half of the rolls.
4. Grill in a preheated panini press until golden brown.

5. Remove from the press and cool for a couple of minutes. Cut into desired shape and serve.

Cannabis Mango-Cashew Fried Rice

Serves: 4

Cooking time: 30 minutes

Ingredients:

- 6 cups cooked brown rice, cold
- 1 cup raw cashew halves
- 2 tablespoons minced ginger
- 2 small Spanish onions, diced
- 1 cup frozen green peas, thawed
- 4 tablespoons low-sodium soy sauce
- 2 teaspoons Worcestershire sauce
- 1 teaspoon tarragon
- 1 teaspoon thyme
- Juice of 2 limes
- 2 mangoes, peeled, pitted, cut into ½ inch pieces
- 8 medium cloves garlic, peeled, minced
- 1 1/2 cups shiitake mushrooms, thinly sliced
- 2 large carrots, diced
- 6 tablespoons canna-extra-virgin olive oil

- 2 tablespoons sesame oil
- 1/2 teaspoon ground turmeric
- Salt to taste
- Pepper to taste

Optional toppings:

- Sesame seeds
- Chopped cilantro
- Sriracha sauce, etc.

Method:

1. Place an iron skillet over medium-low heat. Let the pan heat.
2. Add cashews and roast until light brown in color. Remove the cashews to a plate and set aside to cool.
3. Add 4 tablespoons canna-oil to the skillet and heat. When the oil is heated, add onion, ginger, carrots, and a pinch of salt and mix well. Cook until onions are pink.
4. Push the vegetables to one side of the skillet. Add 2 tablespoons canna-oil. Add half the rice in the center. Press the rice with a spatula. Let it cook for 2 minutes.
5. Now mix all the rice and vegetables in the skillet.
6. Add remaining rice, turmeric, tarragon, thyme, and toss well. Heat thoroughly.
7. Meanwhile, add sesame oil, Worcestershire sauce, and lime juice to a bowl and whisk well. Pour over the rice. Toss well.

Cannabis Cookbook

8. Scatter peas, mangoes, and cashews and toss well.

9. Cook for 3-4 minutes, tossing frequently until peas and mango pieces are warm and the rice is steaming hot.

10. Serve right away topped with optional toppings.

Vegan Cannabis Spaghetti Bolognese

Serves: 8

Cooking time: 20 minutes

Ingredients:

- 4 tablespoon vegan cannabutter or cannabutter if you are not vegan
- 16 ounces baby bella mushrooms
- 4 stalks celery, cut into pieces
- 4 carrots, scrubbed, cut into pieces
- 2 red onions, chopped
- 4 cloves garlic, peeled, minced
- 2 teaspoons crushed red pepper
- 2 tablespoons tomato paste
- 2 pounds pasta, cooked
- 2 tablespoons fennel seeds
- 2 cans whole, peeled plum tomatoes
- 2 teaspoons dried basil
- Salt to taste
- Pepper to taste

Method:

1. Add mushrooms to a food processor bowl. Process until finely chopped.

2. Add carrots, onion, and celery to the food processor and process until finely chopped.

3. Place a large skillet over medium-high heat. Add vegan or normal cannabutter. When butter melts, add all the finely chopped vegetables and mushrooms and stir.

4. Add salt and pepper to taste. Saute until vegetables are cooked.

5. Stir in fennel seeds, garlic, and crushed red pepper. Cook for a minute or until aromatic.

6. Stir in tomato paste, tomatoes, salt, pepper, and basil. Mix well. Cook until the sauce is thick.

7. Serve over cooked pasta.

Weed Quesadillas

Serves: 4

Cooking time: minutes

Ingredients:

- 8 flour tortillas (6 inches each)
- 1 sweet bell pepper, chopped
- 1/2 cup chopped scallions
- 2 cups shredded mozzarella cheese
- 4 tablespoons cannabutter or canna-oil
- 8-12 raw shrimp, chopped
- Salt to taste
- Pepper to taste
- 1 teaspoon oregano or to taste

Method:

1. Place a pan over medium heat. Add canna-oil or butter and heat.
2. Stir in the peppers and cook until slightly tender.
3. Stir in the shrimp and cook for 1-2 minutes. Stir occasionally.
4. Stir in the scallions and cook for 2-3 minutes. Transfer to a bowl.
5. Add some more oil to the pan if required. Place a tortilla on

the pan. Spread 1/4 of the filling on the tortilla. Sprinkle cheese all over the filling.

6. Cover with another tortilla. Press the tortilla all over so that the ingredients stick to each other when cheese melts. Cook until the underside is browned to your liking.

7. Carefully flip sides of the quesadilla. Cook until the underside is browned to your liking.

8. Remove to a plate, cut into 4, and serve.

9. Repeat steps 5-8 and make the other quesadilla.

Cannabis Cookbook

Laid-Back Latkes

Serves: 15-18

Cooking time: 30 minutes

Ingredients:

- 2 cups canna-vegetable oil
- 2 1/2 pounds Russet potatoes, unpeeled, grated
- 1 egg, beaten
- 1/2 teaspoon salt or to taste
- 1 cup cooked rice or couscous or any other grain of your choice
- 1 onion, grated
- 1/4 cup flour or more if required
- Ground pepper, to taste

Method:

1. Place grated potatoes in a bowl of water for a while.
2. Drain the potatoes and place in a colander. Press the potatoes against the colander to remove excess water.
3. Add potatoes, onion, egg, salt, and pepper into a bowl. Mix well. If the mixture is too watery, add some more flour.
4. Place a large pan over medium-high heat. Add canna-vegetable oil and heat. The oil should be well heated but not smoking.

5. Scoop about a heaping tablespoon of pancake mixture into the pan. Flatten to shape into pancake. Place as many as can fit in the pan. Cook until underside is golden brown. Flip sides and cook the other side until it turns golden brown.

6. Remove with a slotted spoon and place on a bed of rice.

7. Repeat with the remaining batter. Serve with sour cream.

CHAPTER THIRTEEN

DINNER RECIPES

Baked Shrimp Scampi

Serves: 3

Cooking time: minutes

Ingredients:

- 1 pound shrimp in shell, peeled, deveined, leave the tails, butterflied
- 1 tablespoon dry white wine
- 6 tablespoons cannabutter, at room temperature
- 2 tablespoons minced shallots
- 1/2 teaspoon minced fresh rosemary leaves
- 1 1/2 tablespoons minced fresh parsley
- 1/8 teaspoon crushed red pepper flakes
- 1 tablespoon fresh lemon juice
- 1/3 cup panko bread crumbs

Cannabis Cookbook

- 1 1/2 tablespoons canna-oil
- Kosher salt to taste
- Pepper to taste
- 2 teaspoons minced garlic
- 1/2 teaspoon grated lemon zest
- Yolk of a medium egg
- Lemon wedges for garnish

Method:

1. Preheat oven to 350°F.
2. Add shrimp to a bowl. Pour wine and oil over it. Sprinkle salt and pepper to taste. Toss well. Set aside for 10 minutes.
3. Add garlic, red pepper flakes, shallots, herbs, butter, lemon juice, lemon zest, panko bread crumbs, yolk, salt, and pepper to a bowl and mix well.
4. Take a small oval dish of about 9-10 inches. Place shrimp on the bottom of the dish, with the curled tail side facing up. Place them in a single layer.
5. Spoon the bread-crumb mixture over the shrimp.
6. Bake at 350°F for about 10-12 minutes or until the mixture is bubbling.
7. For a brown top, broil for a minute.
8. Let cool for a couple of minutes before serving. Garnish with lemon wedges and serve.

Broccoli Cheddar Casserole

Serves: 6-8

Cooking time: 50-60 minutes

Ingredients:

- 30 ounces broccoli, chopped into florets
- 1 1/2 cans cream of mushroom soup
- 3 eggs, beaten
- 6 tablespoons cannabutter
- 1 1/2 cups mayonnaise
- 1 1/2 cups grated sharp cheddar cheese
- 3 cups crushed crackers

Method:

1. Preheat oven to 350°F.
2. Place a pot half filled with water over medium heat. Bring to a boil.
3. Add broccoli and cook until the color changes to bright green.
4. Drain and immerse broccoli in bowl of iced water. Drain after 3 minutes.
5. Place broccoli in a bowl. Add mayonnaise, cheddar cheese, soup, and eggs. Mix well.
6. Grease a casserole dish or baking dish with some oil.

7. Spread the broccoli mixture in the prepared baking dish.

8. Sprinkle crackers over the broccoli layer.

9. Melt butter and pour all over the crackers.

10. Bake at 350°F for about 30-40 minutes or until it turns golden brown.

11. Take it off the oven and cool for 5 minutes.

12. Serve.

Cannabis-Infused Turkey Bolognese

Serves: 3-4

Cooking time: 30 minutes

Ingredients:

- 1/2 box whole-wheat spaghetti
- 1/2 pound ground turkey
- 1/2 can (from a 7.2 ounce can) tomato sauce
- 1 medium onion, finely chopped
- 2 cloves garlic, peeled, minced
- 1/2 cup grated parmesan cheese
- 4-6 drops cannabis tincture
- 1 tablespoon olive oil
- 1/2 can (from a 28 ounce can) chopped tomatoes
- 2 medium carrots, finely chopped
- 1 stalk celery, finely chopped
- 2 tablespoons chopped parsley
- Salt and pepper, to taste

Method:

1. Place a skillet over medium heat and add some oil. When the oil is heated, add carrots, onion, and celery and stir. Cook the

vegetables well.

2. Stir in the ground turkey and garlic and cook until they turn brown.

3. Stir in the tomato sauce and diced tomatoes.

4. Meanwhile, cook spaghetti following the instructions on the package. Drain, retaining 3-4 tablespoons of cooked water.

5. Toss together spaghetti and cannabis tincture and add into the pot. Add the retained water and turkey mixture. Mix well.

6. Garnish with parsley and cheese and serve.

Rasta Pasta

Serves: 4-6

Cooking time: 30 minutes

Ingredients:

- 4 cups shell pasta
- 1 bell pepper of any color, cut into 1/2-inch squares
- 2 cloves garlic, peeled, sliced
- 8 tablespoons flour
- 2-3 teaspoons chopped, fresh dill
- 1 tablespoon soy sauce or to taste
- 3/4 cup canna-milk
- 1 onion, chopped
- 4 tablespoons margarine or canna-margarine
- 1 teaspoon wet mustard
- 6 tablespoons nutritional yeast

Method:

1. Cook pasta following the directions on the package. Drain and set aside.
2. Place a pan over medium-low heat. Add 1 tablespoon margarine and melt.

Cannabis Cookbook

3. Add onion, bell pepper, and garlic and sauté until onion turns translucent. Transfer to the bowl of pasta.

4. Place the saucepan back over heat. Add remaining margarine and melt.

5. Add flour and stir for about a minute. Add canna-milk and stir constantly until well combined. Continue stirring until the sauce thickens.

6. Add in the pasta and vegetables and mix. Heat thoroughly.

7. Serve hot.

Rib Eye with Chimichurri Sauce

Serves: 10

Cooking time: 10 minutes

Ingredients:

For chimichurri sauce:

- 1 cup chopped parsley
- 1/2 tablespoon red wine vinegar
- 3-4 tablespoons chopped parsley
- 4 cannabis fan leaves, finely chopped
- 1/2 teaspoon red chili flakes
- 1 cup canola oil or neutral oil
- 1 teaspoon oregano
- 1/2 tablespoon salt
- 1 cup olive oil

For rib eye:

- 1 bone-in rib-eye steak
- 1 tablespoon kief-infused butter (optional)
- Salt to taste
- Pepper, to taste

- 7-8 tablespoons olive oil

Method:

1. To make chimichurri sauce: Add parsley, salt, vinegar, red chili flakes, cannabis leaves, garlic, oregano, olive oil, and canola oil to a large bowl.

2. Sprinkle salt and pepper generously over the steak. Rub well into the steak. Place steak in a bowl. Do not cover the bowl. Chill for 8-10 hours.

3. Remove steak from the refrigerator and bring to room temperature before cooking.

4. Place a cast iron pan over medium heat. Add oil and heat. Place rib-eye steak in the pan and cook until underside is brown. Flip sides and cook the other side until brown and cooked to liking. It should take approximately 8-10 minutes for medium-rare.

5. Remove steak and place on your cutting board. Let sit for 10 minutes.

6. Slice the steak to desired size

7. Serve steak slices with chimichurri sauce.

Chicken Pic-Canna

Serves: 2

Cooking time: 15 minutes

Ingredients:

- 1 chicken breast, boneless, pounded, halved
- 2 tablespoons canna-oil
- 3-4 tablespoons cannabutter
- 1/4 cup lemon juice
- 3-4 tablespoons capers
- Salt and pepper to taste
- 1/4 cup chicken stock
- 2 tablespoons chopped parsley
- 1/2 cup all-purpose flour

Method:

1. Season the chicken with salt and pepper
2. Place flour on a plate. Coat the chicken all over with flour.
3. Place a pan over medium heat. Add 1 tablespoon cannabutter and 1 1/2 tablespoons canna-oil and heat.
4. Place chicken in the pan and roast for 2-3 minutes. Flip sides and cook the other side for 2-3 minutes. Remove chicken to a plate.

5. Add stock, capers, and lemon juice into the same pan. Place pan over medium heat. When the mixture is hot, add chicken and cook for 4-5 minutes.

6. Remove chicken with a slotted spoon and place on a plate.

7. Add 1 tablespoon canna-oil and remaining cannabutter to the pan. Whisk until butter melts and is well incorporated into the sauce.

8. Spoon the sauce over the chicken. Sprinkle parsley on top and serve.

Chicken Pot-cciatore

Serves: 8

Cooking time: 20-25 minutes

Ingredients:

- 2 fryer chickens, with skin, cut into pieces
- 2 tablespoons cannabutter
- 2 tablespoons olive oil
- 1 cup white wine (optional)
- 5-6 green olives, sliced
- 5-6 black olives, sliced
- Salt and pepper, as per taste
- 2 large onions, cut into 1/2-inch wedges
- 2 cups small cremini mushrooms

Method:

1. Dry the chicken after rinsing by patting with paper towels.
2. Season the chicken.
3. Place a skillet over medium heat and warm the oil and butter.
4. Add chicken pieces in batches and cook until brown. Remove with a slotted spoon and place on a plate lined with paper towels.
5. Add onions into the same pan and cook well.

6. Lower the heat and add the browned chicken back into the pan. Also add mushrooms and cook for 4-5 minutes.

7. Stir in wine and simmer for a couple of minutes. Add olives and mix well. Take off heat; cover and set aside for a few minutes before serving.

Cannabis Chicken Pot Pie

Serves: 8

Cooking time: 45-50 minutes

Ingredients:

- 2 pounds chicken breasts halves, boneless, skinless, chopped into cubes
- 2 cups frozen green peas
- 2 cups carrots, sliced
- 1 large onion, shopped
- 1 stalk celery, sliced
- 2/3 cup cannabutter
- 1 1/3 cups canna-milk
- 2/3 cup all-purpose flour
- 3 1/2 cups chicken broth
- 1/8 teaspoon celery seeds
- Salt to taste
- Pepper to taste
- 4 unbaked pie crusts (9 inches each)
- Water as required

Method:

Cannabis Cookbook

1. Preheat oven to 425°F.

2. Add chicken, peas, carrots, and celery into a saucepan. Place the saucepan over medium heat.

3. Pour enough water to just cover the ingredients in the saucepan.

4. When it begins to boil, cook for about 15 minutes. Remove from heat. Drain the water and put the chicken and vegetables aside.

5. Place a saucepan over medium heat. Add cannabutter. When the butter melts, add onions and sauté until translucent.

6. Add flour, salt, pepper, and celery seeds and sauté for a minute or so until aromatic.

7. Pour the canna-milk and chicken broth slowly, stirring simultaneously.

8. Lower heat and simmer until thick. Turn off the heat.

9. Take 2 of the pie crusts. Divide and keep the chicken and vegetable mixture on it. Spread it all over the crust.

10. Pour the chicken broth mix over it.

11. Cover with the remaining 2 pie crusts. Press the edges of both the crusts together and seal all around.

12. Using a sharp knife, make a few slits on the top crust.

13. Bake at 425°F until the top becomes golden.

14. Remove from the oven and cool.

15. Serve.

Gnocchi in Ganja Butter

Serves: 2

Cooking time: 30-40 minutes

Ingredients:

- 3 medium baking potatoes, skin on, rinsed
- 1 small egg, slightly beaten
- 1 1/2 cups flour or more if required
- 1 tablespoon cannabutter
- 1/2 tablespoon plain olive oil
- 1/2 teaspoon baking powder
- Salt to taste

<u>To serve:</u>

- Grated parmesan cheese or Romano cheese or Asiago cheese, to garnish (optional)
- 2 cloves garlic, minced
- 1 tablespoon cannabutter
- 1/2 tablespoon olive oil or coconut oil
- Red sauce (optional)

Method:

1. Place a pot of water with potatoes and a little salt over medium

heat. Boil until the potatoes are cooked.

2. Peel the potatoes and pass through a sieve so that the potatoes are well mashed and free of lumps. Alternately, mash the potatoes using a potato masher until smooth and free of lumps.

3. Add potatoes, egg, flour, cannabutter, olive oil, baking powder, and salt into a bowl. Mix until well combined and dough is formed. The dough will be bread-dough-like to look at.

4. Take a portion of the dough (cover the remaining dough with a cotton cloth). Roll it between your hands until it is about 5-6 inches long and about an inch in width. Then cut into about 1-1 1/2 inch pieces.

5. Press the pieces with the prongs of the fork to create ridges on the gnocchi.

6. Dust a baking sheet with some flour. Place the cut gnocchi over the baking sheet. Dust the top of the gnocchi with a little flour. Cover with a cotton cloth until ready to use. They may turn slightly gray but that doesn't matter, as they will turn white again after boiling.

7. To boil, place a pot of water over medium heat. Add 1-2 teaspoons salt and 1 tablespoon olive oil.

8. When the water boils, put the gnocchi in the water. Slowly the gnocchi will rise to the top. After it rises, let it boil for 5 minutes.

9. Drain in a colander. Rise **under** until hot water. Transfer to a bowl.

10. To serve: Place a small pan over medium heat. Add canna-

butter and olive oil to the pan. When the butter melts, add garlic and cook until brown.

11. Pour over the gnocchi. Drizzle red sauce over it. Sprinkle cheese on top and serve.

Dope Dumplings Vegetable Casserole

Serves: 2-3

Cooking time: 80-90 minutes

Ingredients:

For veggie casserole:

- 4 ounces parsnips, peeled, sliced
- 1 stick celery, sliced
- 1 ounce butter
- 1/2 can baked beans
- 1/2 ounce flour
- 1/4 cup white wine
- 1/2 teaspoon mixed dried herbs
- 2 carrots, sliced
- 1/2 leek, sliced
- 1 medium onion, chopped
- 1 small clove garlic, crushed
- 1 cup stock
- 3.5 ounces button mushrooms, chopped
- Salt to taste

- Pepper to taste

For dope dumplings:

- 2 ounces self-rising flour
- 1/2 teaspoon mustard powder
- 1/2 ounce butter
- 1 ounce grated cheese
- 1/16 ounce ground cannabis

Method:

1. Place a pan over medium heat. Add butter. When butter melts, add onion and garlic and cook until translucent.
2. Add flour and stir constantly for a couple of minutes. Turn off the heat.
3. Stir in wine and stock.
4. Add rest of the ingredients for casserole and mix well. Transfer to a casserole dish.
5. Place casserole dish over low heat. Cover with lid and cook for 40-50 minutes. Stir occasionally.
6. Meanwhile, make the dumplings as follows: Mix together in a bowl, mustard, flour, and cannabis. Add butter and rub into the mixture. Add cheese and mix well.
7. Sprinkle some water and mix until soft dough is formed.
8. Divide the dough into 5-6 equal portions and shape into balls.

9. Place the dumplings on top of the veggie mixture in the casserole. Cover and continue cooking for another 20-25 minutes.

10. Serve hot.

Classic Cannabis Lasagna

Serves: 3-4

Cooking time: 50-60 minutes

Ingredients:

- 1/2 pound ground turkey or beef
- 1 small onion, finely chopped
- 1/2 can (from a 14.5 ounces can) stewed tomatoes
- 1/2 can (from a 6 ounces can) tomato paste
- 1/2 jar (from a 6 ounce jar) tomato sauce
- 1 large egg
- 1/4 cup ricotta cheese
- 1 teaspoon chopped fresh parsley
- 1/2 teaspoon pepper or to taste
- 4 ounces shredded cheddar cheese
- 4 ounces shredded mozzarella cheese
- 4 ounces grated parmesan cheese
- 3/4 cup cottage cheese
- 1 teaspoon salt
- 1/2 box (from a 8 ounces bag) no-boil lasagna noodles

- 1 clove garlic, minced
- 1 1/2 tablespoons canna-extra-virgin olive oil

Method:

1. Preheat oven to 350°F.
2. Grease a square or rectangular baking dish with some oil.
3. Place a skillet over medium-low heat. Add canna-oil and heat but do not let the oil smoke.
4. Add garlic and onion and sauté for a minute. Add 1/2 teaspoon salt and 1/4 teaspoon pepper. Mix well.
5. Add turkey and cook until brown. Break up the meat as it cooks. Remove any excess fat from the pan.
6. Add tomato sauce, stewed tomatoes, and tomato paste and stir. Cover and continue cooking for 10-12 minutes. Stir every 5 minutes.
7. Add egg into a bowl and whisk well. Add 3/4 cup cottage cheese, 1/4 cup Parmesan cheese, 1/4 cup ricotta cheese, 1 teaspoon chopped parsley, 1/2 teaspoon salt, and 1/4 teaspoon pepper and mix until well incorporated.
8. Add a thin layer of turkey sauce on the bottom of the baking dish.
9. Place a layer of lasagna noodles, slightly overlapping.
10. Spread half the cottage cheese mixture over the noodles followed by half the remaining mozzarella and half the cheddar cheese. Spread some turkey sauce over this layer.
11. Repeat steps 8-9.

12. Sprinkle remaining Parmesan cheese on top.

13. Bake at 350°F for about 25-30 minutes or until thoroughly heated.

Pesto Cannabis Pizza

Serves: 2

Cooking time: 30 minutes

Ingredients:

For pesto:

- 1/2 cup canna-oil
- 1 clove garlic, peeled
- Salt to taste
- 1 cup fresh basil
- 2 tablespoons parmesan cheese, grated

For pizza:

- Pizza dough for 1 small pizza, rolled, or use a pre-cooked pizza base
- 1/4 cup goat cheese, crumbled
- 1/2 small red pepper, diced
- 1 small tomato, sliced
- 1/4 cup shredded mozzarella cheese

Method:

1. Preheat oven to 200°F.
2. Add all the ingredients for pesto into a blender and blend until

smooth.

3. Spread the pesto over the pizza dough.

4. Place red pepper and tomato slices over the pizza.

5. Sprinkle goat cheese and mozzarella cheese.

6. Bake at 200-220°F for about 25-30 minutes. Do not raise the heat, as cannabis will evaporate.

7. Cut into wedges and serve.

Cannabis Cookbook

Cannabis Mashed Potatoes

Serves: 3

Cooking time: 25 minutes

Ingredients:

- 1 1/2 pounds russet potatoes, peeled, cut into small cubes
- 4 tablespoons cannabutter + extra to serve
- Kosher salt to taste
- Freshly ground pepper, as per taste
- 1/4 cup canna-milk
- 1 1/2 tablespoons horseradish
- 1/2 cup sour cream
- Chopped chives, to garnish

Method:

1. Add water to a pot and place the pot over medium heat.
2. Add potatoes and about a teaspoon of salt. Cook until the potatoes are tender.
3. Drain the potatoes and discard the water. Add the potatoes back to the pot. Mash with a potato masher.
4. Add cannabutter and milk to a small saucepan. Place over medium heat. When the mixture is warm, turn off the heat. Pour into the pot. Add salt and pepper. Mix well.

5. Garnish with chives and serve.

Chicken and Vegetables Thai Curry

Serves: 4-5

Cooking time: 40-45 minutes

Ingredients:

- 4-5 tablespoons canna-coconut oil
- 2 cans coconut milk
- 1 medium eggplant, cut into small pieces
- 5 new potatoes, halved
- Cooked basmati rice, to serve
- 4-5 chicken thighs, boneless, skinless, chopped into chunks
- 1 small cauliflower, cut into florets
- 3-4 tablespoons curry paste or to taste
- 3 tablespoons toasted, flaked coconut

Method:

1. Preheat oven to 400°F.
2. Spread eggplant, potatoes, and cauliflower on a greased baking sheet.
3. Roast at 400°F for about 20 minutes.
4. Place a pot over medium flame. Add canna-coconut oil. When

the oil is heated, add chicken and cook until brown.

5. Add the roasted vegetables, curry paste, and coconut milk and mix well. Cook until chicken is done. Stir a couple of times while it is cooking.

6. Garnish with toasted coconut. Serve over rice.

Cannabis Tuna Steaks with Sautéed Spinach

Serves: 4

Cooking time: 25 minutes

Ingredients:

For tuna steaks:

- 4 tuna steaks or ahi or yellowfin steaks (4 ounces each), rinsed
- 4 tablespoons low-sodium soy sauce
- Juice of 2 limes
- 2 teaspoons chopped fresh dill
- Salt and pepper, as per taste
- 3-4 tablespoons canna-extra-virgin olive oil
- 4 cloves garlic, peeled, finely minced
- 2 tablespoons honey
- 2 teaspoons finely minced fresh ginger

For sautéed vegetables:

- 2 tablespoons canna-extra-virgin olive oil
- 2 small white onions, finely diced
- 8 cups baby spinach
- 2 yellow bell peppers, deseeded, finely diced

- 8 cloves garlic, peeled, finely minced
- Salt and pepper, as per taste

Method:

1. Dry the tuna steaks by patting with paper towels. Sprinkle salt and pepper on either side of the steaks.
2. Brush canna-oil over the steaks. Place on a plate and set aside.
3. Take a wide bowl. Add remaining oil, lime juice, soy sauce, garlic, dill, ginger, and honey and mix well.
4. Place steak in this mixture. Coat well on either side. Place the bowl in the refrigerator for 2-3 hours.
5. Place a skillet over medium heat. Add 2 tablespoons canna-oil. When the oil is heated, add onion, bell pepper, salt, and pepper and sauté until onions are pink.
6. Stir in the baby spinach and stir. Cook until spinach wilts. Transfer to a serving platter and set aside.
7. Add remaining oil to the skillet and let heat.
8. Remove steaks from the marinade and place in the skillet. Cook for 4-5 minutes. Flip sides and cook the other side for 4-5 minutes or until the steak is cooked medium-rare to rare.
9. Remove with a slotted spoon and place over the cooked vegetables.
10. You can also add the marinade to a saucepan and place over medium heat. Simmer until thick. Spoon this sauce over the steak and serve.

Lobster Étouffée

Serves: 4

Cooking time: 45 minutes

Ingredients:

- 2 tablespoons oil
- 1/4 teaspoon cannabutter
- 1/4 cup regular butter, divided
- 1/4 cup flour + extra to make paste
- 2 cloves, peeled, minced
- 1/4 teaspoon white pepper
- 1/4 teaspoon black pepper
- 1/2 teaspoon Cajun seasoning
- 2 cups lobster stock
- 1/2 teaspoon salt
- 2 scallions, sliced + extra to garnish
- 1/4 cup green bell pepper, chopped
- 3/4 cup yellow onion, chopped
- 1 bay leaf
- 1/2 can (from a 14.5 ounce can) diced tomatoes

- 2 lobster tails, halved
- 1/4 cup fresh parsley, chopped
- Hot sauce to taste
- Hot cooked rice, to serve

Method:

1. Place a heavy saucepan over low heat. Add 2 tablespoons regular butter and cannabutter. When it melts, add flour and mix well. Stir constantly until aromatic.

2. Stir in the onion, garlic, and green pepper and cook well.

3. Stir in the lobster stock, tomatoes with juice, black pepper, white pepper, Cajun seasoning, hot sauce, parsley, scallion, salt, and cayenne pepper. Mix well.

4. Bring to a boil, stirring constantly. Lower the heat and simmer until thick.

5. Add lobster and simmer for 5 minutes.

6. Turn off the heat. Add 2 tablespoons regular butter and stir until it melts.

7. Sprinkle scallions and parsley and serve over rice.

Cannabis Fish Tacos

Serves: 8

Cooking time: 6 minutes

Ingredients:

- 4 cups sliced green cabbage
- 1 1/2 pounds white-fish fillets
- 1/4 teaspoon salt or to taste
- 2 tablespoons canna-oil
- 1/4 cup salsa
- 1/2 jalapeño, diced
- 1 onion, diced
- 8 corn tortillas
- Lime wedges, to garnish
- 4 teaspoons fajita seasoning
- 2 tablespoons lime juice
- 6 tablespoons chopped fresh cilantro
- 2 tomatoes, diced
- 1 small avocado, peeled, pitted, chopped

Method:

1. Place a pan over medium heat. Spray with cooking spray.

2. Sprinkle fajita seasoning on either side of the fish and rub gently into the fish.

3. Place on a preheated grill and grill for 3 minutes. Flip sides and grill for 3 minutes.

4. Remove from the grill and place on cutting board. Flake the fish into pieces using a fork. Set aside and keep warm in an oven.

5. Add cabbage, salt, lime juice, and cilantro to a bowl. Mix well and set aside. Add canna-oil, onion, tomato, jalapeños, and salsa to a bowl. Mix well.

6. Follow the instructions on the package of the tortillas and warm them.

7. Place tortillas on your countertop. Divide the fish among the tortillas. Divide the salsa mixture among the tortillas. Divide the cabbage mixture among the tortillas.

8. Scatter avocado slices on top.

9. Serve with lime wedges.

CHAPTER FOURTEEN

SOUP AND SALAD RECIPES

Pumpkin Potato Soup

Serves: 4-6

Cooking time: 25 minutes

Ingredients:

- 8 white potatoes, peeled, chopped
- 6 large carrots, sliced
- 2 medium red onions, chopped
- 6 stalks celery, sliced
- 10 cloves garlic, peeled, minced
- 4 cups pumpkin puree
- 8 cups vegetable broth
- 1 teaspoon ground nutmeg
- 4 tablespoons canna-coconut oil

- 2 cups coconut milk
- 2 teaspoons ground cinnamon
- Salt to taste
- Pepper to taste

Optional toppings:

- Pumpkin seeds
- A handful fresh sage, chopped
- Any other toppings of your choice

Method:

1. Place a large Dutch oven or soup pot over medium flame. Add canna-coconut oil. When the oil melts, add onion and potato and sauté for 5 minutes. Stir once during this time.
2. Stir in carrots and celery.
3. Add garlic, salt, and pepper and sauté until aromatic.
4. Stir in pumpkin, broth, coconut milk, and nutmeg.
5. Raise the heat to medium-high heat. When the mixture begins to boil, lower the heat to low and cook until potatoes are soft. Turn off the heat.
6. Blend with an immersion blender until you achieve the consistency you desire.
7. Ladle into soup bowls and serve.

Fresh Tomato Soup

Serves: 3-4

Cooking Time: NA

Ingredients:

- 1 1/2 pounds tomatoes, chopped into chunks
- 1 large clove garlic, peeled, minced
- 1 small red onion, quartered
- Pepper to taste
- Coarse salt to taste
- 1 1/2 tablespoons canna-oil
- 1 teaspoon lemon juice
- 1 1/2 tablespoons balsamic vinegar

To garnish:

- 1 tablespoon feta cheese, crumbled
- 2 tablespoons chopped parsley

Method:

1. Add tomatoes, garlic, salt, pepper, and lemon juice to a bowl and toss well. Cover and set aside for a while to allow the flavors to mingle.
2. Transfer to a blender. Add onion and vinegar and blend until the texture you desire is achieved. Transfer to a bowl. Cover

and place in the refrigerator until ready to use.

3. Ladle into soup bowls. Garnish with feta and parsley and serve.

Cannabis Quinoa Stew

Serves: 8

Cooking time: 30 minutes

Ingredients:

- 1 cup quinoa, rinsed, drained
- 4 cups chopped onions
- 2 cups chopped bell peppers
- 2 cups chopped potatoes
- 3 cups chopped tomatoes
- 2 cups diced zucchini
- 1/2 cup scallions
- 1/2 cup canna-oil
- 2 teaspoons ground coriander
- 2 teaspoons dried oregano
- 2 teaspoons ground cumin
- 6 cups vegetable stock
- 2 tablespoons lemon juice
- 2 teaspoons sea salt or to taste
- 1 teaspoon pepper or to taste

Method:

1. Place a large saucepan or soup pot over medium heat. Add canna-oil and heat. When the oil is heated, add onion and a bit of salt and cook until translucent.

2. Stir in quinoa, bell pepper, zucchini, bell peppers, tomatoes, spices, and stock and mix well. Cover with a lid.

3. When the mixture boils, reduce the heat and cook the vegetables until they are tender.

4. Ladle into soup bowls. Sprinkle scallions on top and serve.

Chili Con Cannabis

Serves: 12-15

Cooking time: 2 1/2 hours

Ingredients:

- 3 cans (15 ounces each) black beans, drained
- 3 cans (15 ounces each) dark red kidney beans, drained
- 3 cans (15 ounce each) black-eyed peas, drained
- 3 medium sweet onions, chopped
- 1/2 cup dry red wine
- 2-3 tablespoons ground cumin
- 2-3 tablespoons dried New Mexico chili flakes
- 2-3 pounds chopped beef (the stir-fry type)
- 3 tablespoons chili powder
- 4-5 tablespoons Lea and Perrins sauce
- 4-5 tablespoons cannabutter
- 1 tablespoon canna-extra-virgin olive oil
- 10-12 cloves garlic, peeled, sliced

Method:

1. Add all the beans to a large pot. Place pot over low heat. When the beans are well heated, add wine, Lea and Perrins sauce,

liquid smoke, cumin, chili powder, and chili flakes.

2. Cover with a lid. Let simmer for about an hour. Stir occasionally.

3. Stir in the onions and tomatoes.

4. Place a skillet over medium heat. Heat oil. Add garlic and fry it well.

5. Add beef and cook until brown. Transfer into the pot. Mix well.

6. Put a lid on the pot and cook on low heat for about 1-1 1/2 hours, stirring occasionally.

7. Add cannabutter and simmer for 25 minutes.

8. Serve in bowls.

Split Pea and Carrot Soup

http://www.weedist.com/2014/09/great-edibles-recipes-medicated-vegan-split-pea-soup/http://www.weedist.com/2014/09/great-edibles-recipes-medicated-vegan-split-pea-soup/

Serves: 3-4

Cooking time: minutes

Ingredients:

- 2 cups dried split peas, rinsed
- 2-2 1/2 cups water
- 2 1/2 cups vegetable broth
- 4 cloves garlic, peeled, minced
- 1 1/2 tablespoon canna-coconut oil
- 1 carrot, cut into bite-size pieces
- 1/2 tablespoon canna-extra-virgin olive oil
- 1 medium onion, finely diced
- 1 1/2-2 tablespoons white miso paste
- 1/2 teaspoon thyme
- Salt and pepper, as per taste
- 1 bay leaf

Method:

1. Place a Dutch oven or soup pot over medium heat. Add canna-extra-virgin olive oil. When the oil is heated, add onion and garlic and cook until onions are translucent.

2. Add carrot and split peas. Season with salt and pepper.

3. Add miso, thyme, canna-coconut oil, and bay leaf and mix well.

4. Stir in broth and water.

5. When mixture begins to boil, lower the heat and cover with a lid. Simmer until split peas are cooked. Stir every 10-12 minutes.

6. Ladle into soup bowls and serve.

Butternut Squash Soup

Serves: 3

Cooking time: 20 minutes

Ingredients:

- 1 tablespoon chopped parsley
- 1/2 tablespoon chopped sage leaves
- 1/2 teaspoon chopped thyme
- 3/4 tablespoon canna-oil or cannabutter
- 3/4 tablespoon cannabutter, to finish
- 1/2 cup celery, chopped
- 1 1/2 pounds butternut squash, peeled, deseeded, chopped
- 1 carrot, chopped
- 1 onion, minced
- 3 teaspoons mild curry powder
- Salt and pepper to taste
- 2 1/2 cups vegetable stock

Method

1. Place a pan over medium flame. Add canna-oil. When the oil is hot, add onions and cook them.
2. Add rest of the ingredients except cannabutter and cook until

the vegetables are soft.

3. When done, blend with an immersion blender until smooth. Taste and adjust the seasonings if necessary

4. Ladle into soup bowls. Add 1/4 tablespoon butter to each bowl.

5. Stir and serve hot.

Medicated French Onion Soup

Serves: 3

Cooking time: 50-60 minutes

Ingredients:

- 1 bay leaf
- 1/2 teaspoon pepper
- 2-3 sprigs thyme
- 3 large Spanish onions, halved, thinly sliced
- 2 tablespoons butter
- 2 tablespoons cannabutter
- 1/4 cup red wine
- 4 cups unsalted beef broth or water
- 1 teaspoon kosher salt
- 1 cup shredded gruyere cheese
- 1/2 French bread baguette, sliced, toasted
- Oyster crackers to serve

Method:

1. Place a soup pot over medium-low heat. Add butter and cannabutter. When it melts, add onions and cook on low until golden brown. Stir every 4-5 minutes. It can take a while to caramelize.

2. Meanwhile, toast the baguette slices on both sides and set aside.

3. Add broth, water, red wine, pepper, and salt into the pot after the onions are caramelized. Mix well.

4. Simmer for about 15 minutes.

5. Set the oven to broiler mode.

6. Take 3 ovenproof bowls. Place a slice of toasted bread in each bowl. Place the bowls on a baking sheet.

7. Pour soup into the bowls. Sprinkle cheese on top.

8. Broil in a preheated oven at 150 degrees F until cheese melts and is browned to your liking.

9. Garnish with a sprig of thyme in each bowl and serve.

Cannabis Cookbook

Cannabis Chicken Noodle Soup

Serves: 8

Cooking time: 30 minutes

Ingredients:

- 1 pound chicken, diced, cooked
- 8 cups chicken broth
- 1 cup chopped carrots
- 2 celery stalks, diced
- 1/2 cup frozen peas, thawed
- 1 cup chopped onions
- Salt to taste
- Pepper to taste
- 12 drops cannabis tincture
- 2 tablespoons butter
- 2 cups vegetable broth
- 1 teaspoon oregano
- 1 teaspoon basil
- 3 cups egg noodles

Method:

Cannabis Cookbook

1. Place a pot over medium flame.

2. Add butter and let melt. When the butter melts, add onions, carrots, and celery and cook well. Stir occasionally.

3. Add chicken, oregano, basil, noodles, peas, cannabis tincture, and chicken stock.

4. Cover the pot and cook until the noodles and veggies are tender.

5. Add salt and pepper and stir.

6. Ladle into soup bowls and serve hot.

Cannabis Cabbage Salad with Sesame-Lime Dressing

Serves: 1-2

Cooking Time: NA

For salad:

- 6 ounces shredded cabbage
- 1/2 cup shredded carrots
- 1 small cucumber, cut into thin strips
- 1/2 tablespoon fresh chopped dill
- 1/2 Granny Smith apple, cored, cut into thin strips
- 1 small red onion, thinly sliced
- 1 tablespoon chives, chopped
- 3 tablespoons walnuts, chopped

For sesame lime dressing:

- 1/4 cup fresh lime juice
- 1 tablespoon honey
- 1/8 teaspoon minced ginger
- 1 1/2 tablespoon canna-extra-virgin olive oil
- 1 tablespoon diced shallots
- 1/2 teaspoon sesame oil

- 1/2 tablespoon apple cider vinegar
- 1 clove garlic, peeled, minced
- 1/2 tablespoon low-sodium soy sauce
- Salt to taste
- Pepper to taste

Method:

1. Add all the ingredients for dressing into a jar. Shake the jar vigorously until well combined. Set aside for a while to allow the flavors to mingle.
2. Add all the ingredients for salad into a bowl and toss well.
3. Pour dressing on top of salad. Toss well and serve.

Butternut Squash and Kale Salad

Serves: 4-6

Cooking time: 30-40 minutes

Ingredients:

For salad:

- 1 large butternut squash, deseeded, peeled, cut into small cubes
- 4 cups chopped kale (discard hard stems or ribs)
- 8 cups spinach
- 1 cup cranberries, dried
- 1/2 cup crumbled feta cheese
- 1/2 cup walnuts, chopped
- Salt and pepper, to taste
- Extra-virgin olive oil, to drizzle

For dressing:

- 4 tablespoons white wine vinegar
- 1/2 cup apple cider vinegar
- 2 tablespoons brown mustard
- Salt to taste
- 1/4 teaspoon pepper or to taste

- 1/2 cup canna-extra-virgin olive oil

- 2 tablespoons honey

- Juice of 2 oranges

- Zest of 2 oranges, grated

- 1/2 teaspoon fresh rosemary

Method:

1. Preheat oven to 400°F.

2. Grease a baking sheet with some oil. Spread the butternut squash over it.

3. Season with salt and pepper. Drizzle oil over it.

4. Bake at 400°F for about 30-40 minutes or until cooked through and golden brown. Do not overcook. Stir a couple of times while baking.

5. Set aside the butternut squash to cool.

6. Meanwhile, make the dressing as follows: Add all the ingredients for dressing except oil into a blender. Blend until smooth. With the blender running, drizzle canna-oil in a thin stream through the feeder tube of the blender. Blend on low until the mixture is emulsified.

7. Pour dressing over the salad. Toss well and serve.

Cranberry Walnut Salad

Serves: 2

Cooking Time: NA

Ingredients:

For salad:

- 4 cups baby spinach
- 3 tablespoons crumbled feta cheese
- 1/4 cup crushed walnuts
- 1 Fuji apple, cored, thinly sliced
- 3 tablespoons dried cranberries

For apple cider cannabis vinaigrette:

- 2 tablespoons canna-extra-virgin olive oil
- 1/4 teaspoon Dijon mustard
- 1/8 teaspoon garlic powder
- 1/8 teaspoon dried basil
- 1/8 teaspoon dried oregano
- Salt to taste
- Freshly ground pepper to taste
- 2 tablespoons apple cider vinegar

- 1/2 teaspoon light brown sugar
- 1/4 teaspoon pepper or to taste

Method:

1. Make the dressing as follows: Add all the ingredients for dressing except oil into a blender. Blend until smooth. With the blender running, drizzle canna-oil in a thin stream through the feeder tube of the blender. Blend on low until the mixture is emulsified.

2. Transfer to a bowl. Cover and set aside for a while to allow the flavors to mingle.

3. Add all the ingredients for salad into a bowl and toss well.

4. Pour dressing on top of salad. Toss well and serve.

Kale Salad with Cannabutter Vinaigrette

Serves: 2

Cooking time: 10 minutes

Ingredients:

For the salad:

- 1/2 pound Tuscan kale, torn or chopped into bite-size pieces (discard hard ribs and stems)
- 1/4 cup almonds, slivered and toasted

For vinaigrette:

- 3 tablespoons cannabutter
- 3 tablespoons unsalted butter
- Salt to taste
- 3 tablespoons sherry vinegar or red wine vinegar

Method:

1. For brown butter vinaigrette: Place a small pan over high heat. Add unsalted butter and cook until brown.
2. Stir in cannabutter. When it melts, turn off the heat.
3. Stir in the vinegar and salt to taste.
4. Place kale in a bowl. Sprinkle almonds on top. Pour vinegar over it. Toss well and serve.

Cannabis-Infused Greek Salad

Serves: 2-3

Cooking time: 12-15 minutes

Ingredients:

For salad:

- 1/2 tablespoon extra-virgin olive oil
- 1/2 teaspoon fresh oregano, finely chopped
- 1 chicken breast, boneless
- 1/2 red onion, thinly sliced
- 1/2 green pepper, chopped
- 1 small tomato, chopped
- 1/2 cucumber, sliced
- 1/2 head romaine lettuce
- 3 ounces canned black olives, pitted
- 1/2 cup crumbled feta cheese
- Salt to taste
- Pepper to taste

For dressing:

- 1 tablespoon red wine vinegar

- 2 tablespoons extra-virgin olive oil
- 2 teaspoons lemon juice
- 4-5 drops cannabis tincture

Method:

1. Place a skillet over medium-high heat. Add oil and heat. Add chicken and cook until the underside is golden brown. Flip sides and cook until golden brown on both sides.

2. Remove chicken from the pan and place on cutting board. When cool enough to handle, cut into slices.

3. Meanwhile, add all the ingredients for dressing into a small jar. Fasten the lid. Shake the jar vigorously until well combined.

4. Add lettuce, olives, red onion, cucumber, green pepper, and tomato into a bowl and toss well.

5. Drizzle the dressing on top. Toss well.

6. Divide into plates. Place chicken on top. Sprinkle oregano and feta cheese on top and serve.

CHAPTER FIFTEEN

DESERT RECIPES

Pineapple Express Upside-Down Cake

Serves: 4-5

Cooking time: 45 minutes

Ingredients:

- 3-4 canned pineapple slices, drained
- 1/4 cup + 1 tablespoon firmly packed light brown sugar
- 1 cup granulated sugar
- 6 tablespoons cannabutter, at room temperature
- 1 cup cake flour
- 1/2 teaspoon salt
- 3/4 tablespoon dark rum
- 1 egg
- 6 tablespoons milk

- 3/4 teaspoon vanilla extract
- 1/2 teaspoon + 1 pinch baking powder
- 3-4 maraschino cherries

Method:

1. Preheat oven to 350°F.
2. Place rack in the lower third position in the oven.
3. Grease a small round pie pan of about 6-7 inches diameter with some oil or butter.
4. Place pineapple slices on the bottom of the pan. Arrange them so they're not overlapping.
5. Add 3 tablespoons cannabutter, 1/4 cup light brown sugar, and 1/4 cup granulated sugar into a saucepan.
6. Place the saucepan over medium heat. When butter melts, turn off the heat and stir until sugar is dissolved completely.
7. Pour this mixture all over the pineapple slices in the pan.
8. Sift cake flour, baking powder, and salt in a bowl.
9. Add rum, milk, 1 tablespoon brown sugar, and vanilla into a bowl and whisk well.
10. Beat together 3 tablespoons cannabutter and remaining sugar with an electric mixer until fluffy. Add egg and beat well. Add vanilla extract.
11. Set the mixer on low and add flour and milk, a little at a time, and beat until just combined (only fold and do not overbeat).

Cannabis Cookbook

12. Pour into the dish, over the pineapple slices.

13. Bake at 350°F for about 35-40 minutes or until done.

14. Turn off the oven and let the dish remain in the oven for 10 minutes.

15. Remove from the oven and let cool for 12-15 minutes. Loosen the edges and invert on a plate.

16. Cut into 4-5 slices. Place a cherry in the center of each slice and serve.

Banana Marijuana Ice Cream

Serves: 12

Cooking time: 5 minutes

Ingredients:

- 1/2 stick butter
- 10 tablespoons sugar
- 1/8 teaspoon salt
- 6 tablespoons rum
- 0.7 ounces finely ground marijuana
- 36 ounces cream
- 30 ounces bananas, peeled
- 10 tablespoons honey

Method:

1. Add cream to a saucepan. Place saucepan over medium heat. When the cream is well heated but not boiling, stir in the marijuana. Mix well and turn off the heat.

2. Add butter, sugar, and salt to another saucepan. Place over low heat. When butter melts, turn off the heat and stir until well combined.

3. Add the cream mixture into the butter saucepan and whisk well.

4. Mash the bananas in a bowl. Pour in the cream mixture and

mix well.

5. Add honey and rum and beat until well combined.

6. Transfer into a freezer-safe container. Cover with a lid and freeze. After 3 hours, remove the ice cream from the freezer and transfer the ice cream into a chilled bowl.

7. Whisk well. Cover with cling film and freeze until firm. 30 minutes before serving, remove the ice cream from the freezer and place in the refrigerator.

8. Scoop and serve.

Dank Cheesecake

Serves: 8

Cooking time: 60 minutes

Ingredients:

- 2/3 cup cannabutter, softened
- 4 packages (8 ounces each) cream cheese, softened, at room temperature
- 2/3 cup milk
- 1 cup sour cream
- 4 tablespoons all-purpose flour
- 2 premade graham cracker crusts (9 ounces each)
- 1 1/2 cups white sugar
- 4 eggs
- 3 teaspoons vanilla extract

Method:

1. Preheat oven to 350°F.
2. Add cannabutter, cream cheese, and sugar to a mixing bowl. Beat until smooth and frothy.
3. Beat in the milk, vanilla, sour cream, eggs, and flour.
4. Divide and pour into the crusts.
5. Bake at 350°F for about 1 hour.

6. Let sit for 5 hours inside the oven.

7. Chill for about 2-3 hours.

8. Slice and serve.

Marijuana Chocolate Chip Cookies

Serves: 20-30

Cooking time: 10-12 minutes

Ingredients:

- 5 cups flour
- 2 teaspoons salt
- 2 ounces butter
- 12 ounces cannabutter
- 2 teaspoons baking soda
- 2 big cups brown sugar (do not pack)
- 1 1/2 cups sugar
- 4 eggs
- 2 teaspoons vanilla extract
- 3 1/2 cups chocolate chips

Method:

1. Preheat oven to 375°F.
2. Add flour, baking soda, and salt to a bowl and mix until well combined.
3. Beat together cannabutter, brown sugar, and sugar with an electric beater on high until fluffy. Add vanilla extract. Beat well.
4. Add the eggs, one at a time and beat well each time.
5. Add flour and mix well.
6. Add chocolate chips and mix well.
7. Scoop out cookies and place on a lined baking sheet. Leave a gap between the cookies (about an inch).
8. Bake at 375°F for 10-12 minutes.
9. Remove the baking sheet from the oven. Loosen the cookies with a metal spatula after 5 minutes
10. Cool well.
11. Serve or store in an airtight container.

Cannabis Cookbook

Cannabis Caramels

Serves: 35-40

Cooking time: 15 minutes

Ingredients:

- 2 cups cannabutter
- 1/4 teaspoon salt
- 2 cans (14 ounces each) sweetened condensed milk
- 4 1/2 cups brown sugar
- 2 cups light corn syrup
- 2 teaspoons vanilla extract

Method:

1. Add butter, salt, and brown sugar to a pan. Place pan over medium heat. Mix well.
2. Add light corn syrup and stir. Cook for 3-4 minutes.
3. Stir in the milk. Cook until the candy feels like a firm ball when you touch it.
4. Turn off the heat. Add vanilla and stir.
5. Transfer to a rectangular pan. Cool completely. Cut into pieces. Wrap and store.

Pumpkin Cheesecake Smoothie

Serves: 4

Cooking Time: NA

Ingredients:

- 4 cups vanilla almond milk
- 4 tablespoons Ancient Delight Superfood Mix*
- 1/2 teaspoon pure almond extract
- 1/2 teaspoon pure vanilla extract
- 4 tablespoons canned pumpkin
- 2 heaping tablespoons canna-coconut oil
- 2 bananas, sliced, frozen
- 1/4 cup raw cashews
- 4 tablespoons cream cheese

<u>Optional toppings:</u>

- Ground cinnamon
- 4 cinnamon sticks
- Crushed graham crackers

Method:

1. *If you do not have Ancient Delight Superfood Mix, mix together 1/2 teaspoon ground nutmeg, 1 teaspoon ground

cinnamon, 2 tablespoons chia seeds, and 1/2 teaspoon ground ginger in a bowl.

2. Add the smoothie ingredients to the blender and blend until smooth.

3. Pour into glasses. Top with optional toppings and serve.

Marbled Marijuana Brownie Bars

Serves: 6-8

Cooking time: minutes

Ingredients:

- 1 package (8 ounces) cream cheese, softened
- 1 tablespoon granulated sugar
- 1/2 package (from a 21 ounce package) brownie mix. Make the batter following the instructions on the package, but use canna-oil or cannabutter instead of oil or butter
- 1 egg
- 1/2 teaspoon vanilla extract

Method:

1. Preheat oven to 350°F.
2. Add cannabutter, cream cheese, eggs, vanilla, and sugar to a mixing bowl. Beat with an electric mixer until smooth and creamy.
3. Grease a small baking dish with cooking spray. Spread half the prepared brownie batter in the dish.
4. Spread cream cheese mix over the batter. Spread remaining batter over the cream cheese layer.
5. Bake at 350°F for 30-40 minutes.
6. Take out of the oven and cool completely.

7. Cut into bars and serve.

No-Bake Almond-Butter Canna-Cookies

Serves: 12-15

Cooking time: 5 minutes

Ingredients:

- 2 tablespoons unrefined canna-coconut oil
- 6 tablespoons unrefined coconut oil
- 1/2 cup grade B maple syrup or honey
- 1 cup creamy almond butter
- 1/4 teaspoon sea salt
- 3/4 cup cocoa powder
- 2 cups thick rolled oats
- Sea flakes, to top
- A handful almonds, chopped, to top

Method:

1. Place a sheet of parchment paper over a large baking sheet.
2. Add coconut oil and canna-coconut oil into a saucepan. Place saucepan over medium heat. When the oils melt, add cocoa powder, maple syrup, and almond butter. Mix until well combined. Turn off the heat.
3. Add rolled oats and salt and mix well.
4. Scoop the mixture onto the baking sheet. Flatten slightly.

5. Top with sea salt flakes and almonds.

6. Chill until firm.

7. Serve. Leftovers can be stored in an airtight container. Place in the refrigerator until ready to use.

Cannabis Peanut Butter Fudge

Serves: 18-20

Cooking time: 2-4 minutes + 1 hour cooling

Ingredients:

- 2 cups unsalted cannabutter
- 2 cups smooth natural peanut butter
- 2 teaspoon vanilla extract
- 1/2 teaspoon salt
- 2 pounds powdered sugar

Method:

1. Add cannabutter, peanut butter, and salt to a microwave safe dish. Microwave on high for 2 minutes or until completely melted. Stir a couple of times while melting.
2. Add vanilla and sugar powder. Mix well.
3. Line a baking pan with parchment paper.
4. Spread the peanut butter mixture into the pan. Spread evenly with an offset spatula.
5. Cover the pan with plastic wrap. Chill for about an hour.
6. Cut into 1-inch squares.
7. Can last for a week in the refrigerator.

Piña Co-Canna Pie Cake

Serves: 10

Cooking Time: NA

Ingredients:

- 3/4 cup graham crumbs
- 1 package (8 ounces) cream cheese, softened
- 1/4 cup Cool Whip
- 1/4 cup cherries, diced
- 1/4 cup cannabutter, softened
- 1/4 cup cream of coconut
- 1/4 cup pineapple, crushed, diced
- 1/2 cup shredded coconut

Method:

1. Add cannabutter and graham crackers to a bowl and stir well.
2. Take a small baking pan and place the cracker crumb mixture in it. Spread evenly onto the bottom of the pan. Press well.
3. Add cream cheese and cream of coconut into a bowl and beat until creamy.
4. Fold in the Cool Whip, cherries, and pineapple.
5. Spoon the mixture on the cracker crust.
6. Sprinkle shredded coconut on top.

7. Place the pie cake in the refrigerator for 2-3 hours.

8. Slice and serve.

Raspberry Peach Cannabis Cobbler

Serves: 3-4

Cooking time: minutes

Ingredients:

For cobbler:

- 1 cup sliced fresh peach, peeled, pitted
- 1 1/2 cups fresh raspberries
- 3 tablespoons sugar
- 1 tablespoon lemon juice or to taste
- 1/2 tablespoon all-purpose flour
- Pinch ground cinnamon

For cobbler topping:

- 2 tablespoons cannabutter, melted
- 3 tablespoons packed brown sugar
- 1/4 teaspoon crushed pecans or almonds
- Large pinch ground cinnamon
- 1/3 cup rolled oats
- 1/2 teaspoon pure vanilla extract
- 1/8 teaspoon salt

Cannabis Cookbook

- 3 tablespoons all-purpose flour

Method:

1. Preheat oven to 350°F.

2. To make filling: Add peach to a bowl. Sprinkle sugar, flour, cinnamon, and lemon over it. Mix well.

3. Add raspberries and stir until well combined. Do not overmix.

4. Transfer to a greased baking dish. Spread evenly.

5. To make cobbler topping: Add brown sugar, flour, oats, vanilla, cinnamon, pecans, and salt to a bowl and mix well.

6. Add melted cannabutter and mix well.

7. Spread this mixture over the fruit filling.

8. Bake at 350°F for 30-40 minutes.

9. Remove from the oven and cool for a few minutes.

10. Serve warm with vanilla ice cream if desired.

Cannabis Cookbook

Pot Pastelitos

Serves: 18

Cooking time: 30 minutes

Ingredients:

- 2 premade sheets of puff pastry dough
- Fruit filling of your choice
- Canna-honey, as required
- Simple syrup to serve

Method:

1. Preheat oven to 350°F.
2. Place the puff pastry sheets on your countertop.
3. Cut each of the sheets into 9 equal squares.
4. Place a teaspoon of the fruit filling in the middle of each square. Drop 3-4 drops of canna-honey over it.
5. Bring 2 opposite corners together and press them together so you have puff pastry triangles with fruit filling in the center.
6. Press the corners with fork.
7. Place the triangles on a baking sheet. Brush simple syrup over the triangles.
8. Bake at 350°F for 20 to 30 minutes.
9. Remove from the oven and cool.

10. Serve warm or cold.

11. Leftovers can be stored in an airtight container.

CONCLUSION

I want to thank you once again for purchasing this book. I hope it proved to be an enjoyable and informative read.

In this book, you were given all the information that you need so that you can start cooking with cannabis. Apart from this, you were also given all the information that you will need to fully understand the benefits that cannabis offers, along with the associated risks. Armed with the information given in this book, you will be able to decide about the different things you must remember while cooking with cannabis. Regardless of whether you are thinking about cooking with cannabis or are already cooking with cannabis, there are certain mistakes that a lot of people make. By following the simple steps and tips given in this book, you can avoid those mistakes and start cooking with cannabis like a pro!

The recipes for cannabis edibles given in this book are quite easy to understand and simple to follow. Well, cooking with cannabis isn't that complicated, is it? All that you need to do is gather the right ingredients and follow the recipes given in this book. Make sure that you are cautious while cooking with cannabis. Also, it is always a good idea to consult a medical practitioner before you start consuming any cannabis-infused products. Another thing that you cannot afford to ignore is verifying whether using cannabis is legal in your area or not!

Thank you, and all the best!

www.ingramcontent.com/pod-product-compliance
Lightning Source LLC
Chambersburg PA
CBHW071157070526
44584CB00019B/2833